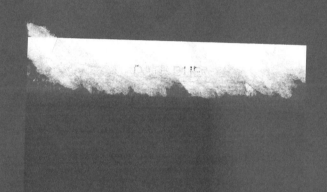

Inspiration

Inspiration

PROFILES OF BLACK WOMEN CHANGING OUR WORLD

CRYSTAL McCRARY

and

NATHAN HALE WILLIAMS

*

Photography by

LAURI LYONS

Stewart, Tabori & Chang
New York

Contents

Majora Carter

55

Debra Martin Chase

65

Misty Copeland

73

Ruby Dee

81

Marian Wright Edelman

87

Iman

135

Judith Jamison

147

Gayle King

155

Patti LaBelle

165

Debra L. Lee

171

Betye Saar

215

Nina Shaw

221

Raven-Symoné

229

Susan L. Taylor

235

Venus Williams

245

Inspiration allows thirty exceptional people to tell their unique stories. Each of these women takes us on her life journey, describing the people, the teachings and the circumstances that shaped her. We see the role that family, culture, community and mentorship play, as well as the influence of dreams, ambitions and ideas.

These women have achieved extraordinary success, sometimes in the face of seemingly insurmountable circumstances. Even more important, each one has attributes of character — integrity, courage, energy, commitment, faith, drive — that illustrate how talent and character come together to create a rich and fulfilling life. The results are astonishing: world-class music, magnificent works of art and prosperous, expanding companies.

I am delighted that Morgan Stanley Smith Barney has been able to play a small role in making this project a reality, and I hope you enjoy and find inspiration in these stories.

Andy Saperstein,
Managing Director, Head of Wealth Management Group
Morgan Stanley Smith Barney

For my Inspirations and the Loves of my Life:

My parents, Thelma and Magellan: you got all the important things right.
My children, Cole and Ella: you give meaning and joy to it all.
My sister, Ruthie: you make sense of it all.
My man, Raymond: you make it all worthwhile.

*

Introduction

In 1987 I was given a copy of Brian Lanker's *I Dream a World* by one of my mother's best friends, Rose Swanson. I will never forget seeing the black-and-white image of Septima Clark on the cover. Where had she come from? My curiosity was ignited. She was so dignified, so proud, so purposeful, and so real—it was a beautifully honest photograph. I had never seen such a book before. I was invigorated. Fine. Beautiful. Bold. Brilliant. Colored women. Black women. African American women. (Ain't they bad!) I was overwhelmed by these women. I was imbued with a sense of possibility. The women of *I Dream a World* were women I had seen in magazines and books, women I had heard sing or speak, women whose writings I had read, women whom I had never heard of before, women I had dreamed about. I was in awe.

I Dream a World was a gift for my graduation from Mercy, an all-girls Catholic high school in Farmington Hills, Michigan. It was fitting that Mrs. Swanson gave it to me, as she was the sort of woman who celebrated black sisterhood and strong women. Mrs. Swanson was an intelligent, beautiful woman, a wife, mother, Detroit public school teacher, proud member of Delta Sigma Theta, and dedicated member of our community. She very well could have been one of the women profiled in *I Dream a World*, as could many of the women who made up the tapestry of my childhood.

I grew up in downtown Detroit and went to Christ Church every Sunday with my family. My parents, Magellan and Thelma McCrary, were born in Georgia and Alabama, respectively, and their families migrated north in the twenties to find work. After coming home from World War II, my dad got a job with Ford Motor Company, and he worked there for forty years. My mother was a Detroit public school teacher and principal for more than forty years. We were not wealthy by any means, but my parents worked hard, saved their money, and made sure my sister and I felt secure, had good values, and received an excellent education. A tall, elegant woman, my mother would neatly dress for work every morning before making breakfast wearing one of her many aprons. She would fix my dad the brown-bag lunch he took to work every day. She would then get my sister and me off to school, head to work herself, then return home, cook dinner, do homework with us, bathe us, read us a story, put us to bed, and somehow bake cookies, rolls, and cakes in her spare time. She did this every day and every night without fail. Honesty, hard work, kindness, and love were the hallmarks of my childhood. And there were other African American women in my community, mothers of my childhood friends, who similarly cared for their families: Mrs. Whatley, Mrs. Pitts, Mrs. Danley, Dr. Doss, Mrs. Mackey, Mrs. Dodd, Mrs. Sims, Judge Diggs, and so many others.

These black women informed my early perception of motherhood and community. I marvel now when I reflect on my mother and these other women, because they were fierce. They did it all without thinking twice. They did what needed to be done to make better lives for their children. With few material possessions, they took care of their households, husbands, and children while remaining dignified and beautiful. They took pride not only in their families but also in their own womanhood. I am indebted to them. I feel a responsibility to their legacy and the legacies of so many before and after them, a responsibility to set the record straight. I feel a responsibility to honor their memories and the sacrifices they made for their children and communities.

I received *I Dream a World* as I was about to head off to college at the University of Michigan. For the first time in my life, I contemplated who I wanted to be as a woman. Like many seventeen-year-olds, I had no idea what I wanted to do with my life other than get through college and perhaps do something "creative," whatever that meant. Over the course of my freshman year and beyond, I found myself returning to the stories and images of the women in *I Dream a World*. I found comfort, guidance, and inspiration in their lives. Each of those women was like a little treasure to be savored and protected. As it happened, my creativity took a slight detour: I graduated, went to law school, and joined a large New York City law firm before leaving to finally pursue that career in the arts. I started writing novels and producing television shows and film, and I made sure to feature strong black women in some shape or form. It was both a passion and an obsession of mine.

I Dream a World left an indelible mark on my mind and my being. Every step, every experience in my life, personal and professional, has led me to the book you are now holding. Having the supreme privilege not only of interviewing these extraordinary women and hearing their remarkable stories, but also of crafting a narrative capturing the spirit of their journeys, has been more than just an honor. It has been a defining experience in my life. All the women have been incredibly generous in what they have shared of their lives: their stories, advice, pitfalls, passions, inspirations, and, most valuable, their time. I have been so humbled by and grateful for their generosity of spirit. These are extremely busy women, but they took the time to be a part of *Inspiration*. And since I began this project, not a day has gone by when I haven't thought about some gem that these thirty extraordinary women shared. My life is fuller and richer from hearing their stories. These women are gifts to us all.

In the course of interviews and photo shoots, I watched Judith Jamison sway and smile and emote excellence while the next generation of Ailey dancers were transfixed in her regal presence, imagining perhaps that their paths might mirror hers. I listened to Marian Wright Edelman drop painful knowledge about the cradle-to-prison pipeline that is plaguing our black sons and daughters in this country, and I was rapt as Susan Taylor's silky voice told me about the beautiful black women she saw on college campuses in the sixties and seventies, who had never heard anyone call them pretty before. I was grateful to enter Betye Saar's Hollywood Hills art studio and be surrounded by her "found" treasures, which each hold a magical story waiting to be told by her hands and her heart. I listened to Shonda Rhimes plainly state the truth that all writers must understand in order to be writers: "You must write every day." And I learned the many lives and lessons of Bethann Hardison, especially the importance of running one's own race. Thelma Golden shared with me her deep passion for art, which began when she was a young girl, and Janice Bryant Howroyd—one of the world's most successful businesswomen—shared what she considers her greatest achievement: learning to love herself the way God intended. Mary J. Blige told me she needed to learn to get out of her own way before life really started opening up for her. I was touched by the joyous addiction to life that Gayle King radiates with every word she speaks, and by her reminder to all women that there is a big pie out there, enough for each of us. I listened to Iman's stories about recognizing her self-worth and fighting to ensure others were aware of theirs. I saw Keke Palmer, through all her early successes, be constantly respectful to her mother and father and give praise to God. I witnessed Ruby Dee soulfully recite poetry and tales alone onstage at the Ossie Davis Theater with only a chair and her extraordinary talent as her companions.

To hear these women share the unfolding of their destinies, through triumph and tragedy, to witness the possibilities that these women turned into realities, has been both humbling and inspiring. They made me *feel*, again and again. They reminded me that excellence prevails, that standards still exist, that hard work does indeed pay off, and that staying true to oneself is ultimately the measure of one's success and, more important, one's fulfillment. The women of *Inspiration* embody a commitment to the ideals of truth and beauty. They are the women I want my daughter, Ella, to emulate as she forges her own path in the world. They are the sort of women I hope my son, Cole, will seek as a partner. They deserve to be honored.

We have made great gains in recent decades in acknowledging and celebrating the accomplishments of all women, regardless of race. Indeed, women now hold leadership positions in business, politics, athletics, academics, and entertainment. The women of *Inspiration* stand on their own merits and are successful by any standard. Without question, their examples will inspire and move us for generations to come. They, along with other strong, dignified, compassionate, and unsung heroic women, beginning with my dear mother, have allowed me to be the woman I am today. They have spent a little time with me and have allowed me the privilege of sharing their legacy with you. It is on their shoulders that I stand. It is their inspiration that moves us forward.

Michelle Obama

Before she became the First Lady of the United States, Michelle Robinson Obama attended Princeton University and Harvard Law School. She is the mother of two daughters, Malia and Sasha. As First Lady, she has supported military families, become a fashion icon, and planted a garden on the White House lawn. Her Let's Move! campaign is working hard to combat childhood obesity.

✸

When I think about what First Lady Michelle Obama represents to this country, I cannot help but imagine what her foundation and journey must have been like as she was growing up on the South Side of Chicago, in a one-bedroom apartment where she and her brother, Craig, slept in the living room with a sheet serving as a makeshift room divider. She was raised by two hardworking, devoted parents whose priorities were clearly family, honesty, and education. Her upbringing by a strong mother and father who emphasized core values of a solid work ethic and pride is not dissimilar to most black people's history in this country.

When I think of Mrs. Obama in the context of how African American women are perceived today, I think of the inspiring women in my own midwestern community (women much like Marian Robinson, Mrs. Obama's mother) and women in communities across America, who in the face of adversity have raised generations of African Americans with commitment and grace. Mrs. Obama has described her parents as being "the warmest, hardest-working people I have ever known," and clearly she has been the beneficiary of the values they instilled. Michelle Obama has made us all extremely proud in representing not only the United States of America but also her own family, for she is an extraordinary woman under the strictest of scrutiny. She has demonstrated excellence from an early age, having learned to read at home by the age of four, skipped second grade, excelled academically, and attended Princeton University and then Harvard Law School. Her brother, Craig Robinson, has said, "Without being immodest, Michelle and I were always smart, were always driven, and were always encouraged to do the best you can do, not just what's necessary. And when it came to going to schools, we all wanted to go to the best schools we could."

After graduating from two of the nation's top universities, Mrs. Obama went on to have a successful career as an associate at the Chicago law firm of Sidley Austin and then as a public servant for the city of Chicago and an associate dean at the University of Chicago, before becoming an executive at the University of Chicago Medical Center. Through it all she has managed to be a devoted wife and mother, while surviving a presidential campaign in which her husband made history by becoming the first African American president of the United States. She was able to kick off her own initiatives in support of military families, to start the Let's Move! campaign combating childhood obesity, to help working women balance career and family, and to encourage national service. She has stepped into her unprecedented role as the first African American First Lady with dignity, intelligence, and candor under the media's relentless glare. Mrs. Obama has remained steady, poised, and thoughtful, with a quiet, commanding presence — she is clear on her goals and earnest in her executions.

Much has been written about Mrs. Obama helping to change the perception of African American women in this country and to eradicate age-old stereotypes we've all seen played over and over in the media — gross mischaracterizations of us as "angry black women," "sassy," "mammies," "aggressive," "controlling," and "emasculating." Such descriptions are dated in their attempt to minimize us and insulting in their inaccuracy. Yet they have persisted and have been exacerbated in recent years. The consistent negative images of African American women in the media — from the slate of reality shows depicting us at our worst to music videos that objectify and debase us to daily news feeds of drugged-out, screaming black women running through the streets in bathrobes — have served to reinforce what we know is not the truth of us. Such imagery has never been the truth of who black women are as mothers, wives, grand-mothers, sisters, aunts, or human beings. Mrs. Obama is acutely aware of the impor-tance of portrayals of black women and the need for positive representation. She has said of her March 2009 *Vogue* magazine cover, "While I don't consider myself a fash-ionista, I thought it was good for my daughters and little girls just like them, who haven't seen themselves represented in these magazines, hopefully to talk more broadly about what beauty is, what intelligence is, what counts." Without heavy-handedness, Mrs. Obama is ever conscious of what is important and what is just, particularly as it relates to African American girls' perceptions and sense of possibility for themselves and their futures.

The First Lady's embodiment of humanity and excellence invalidates stereotypes that have plagued black women for years. And what is interesting in the larger dis-cussion of what Mrs. Obama's image means to America is that her persona is actu-ally closer to the reality of black women than not. We are, just as our ancestors were, devoted mothers, principled, spiritual, supportive of our communities, and proud. The stereotypes of black women were never representative of who we are. We have never been what the larger society attempted to force upon us by way of unflattering traits. The dignity, pride, and grace that the world has observed in Michelle Obama since she emerged on the national scene should absolutely be celebrated, emulated, and praised. Yet such admirable traits of the First Lady do not translate into a "recasting" or "rede-fining" of African American women. Rather, their recognition is an acknowledgment of what we have always known to be true about whence we came. Mrs. Obama, in all her grace, is the manifestation of a long history of courageous, intelligent black women upon whose shoulders she stands. She is the embodiment of an enduring struggle of African American women throughout this country's history—great women who helped shape America, from abolitionists Sojourner Truth and Harriet Tubman to writer Phillis Wheatley; to Spelman College founders Sophia B. Packard and Har-riet E. Giles; to entrepreneur and philanthropist Madam C. J. Walker; to activists Ella Baker, Rosa Parks, and Myrlie Evers-Williams; to Vivian Malone; to Coretta Scott King; to Dr. Betty Shabazz; to Marian Robinson; to all the leaders and founders of this country's black sororities and sisterhoods; to all the black women who deprived themselves daily to ensure opportunities for their children; and to all the fine black women who got dressed in their Sunday best without fail no matter how difficult the week to give praise to all the black Women of Inspiration in this book and across the United States of America and the world. On their shoulders Mrs. Obama stands. On their shoulders we all stand. This is the stock from which we hail. This is our history of survival and triumph.

The dignified, strong black woman whom President Obama has referred to as his "rock" is the reality. Mrs. Obama may be the world's most visible African American woman and may thus seem remote from reality, but at her core she represents who we are as black women in this country. The character Mrs. Obama possesses and displays is not an anomaly for African American women. Rather, it represents the best of us, the possibility of us, the beauty of us, the hope of us, the expectation of us, the truth of us.

Inspiration

Laila Ali

Laila Ali is a former boxer and the daughter of the famed world champion and entrepreneur Muhammad Ali. She was named Super Middleweight Champion by the International Boxing Association in 2002 and by the International Women's Boxing Federation in 2005. She has three stepchildren and two children.

✳

I grew up in Los Angeles, California, in a neighborhood called Hancock Park, where my parents were married. When I think about my childhood, what stands out most are the summers, when my dad would pile me and my six sisters into his brown Rolls-Royce and take us for a ride on Wilshire Boulevard with the top down. He'd pull over to the side of the road to give homeless people money or to sign autographs. He loved to be noticed. I remember not really understanding why people loved him so much but knowing that he was very special. My mom has always been a very sophisticated, impeccably dressed woman—very gorgeous. In my eyes, she was the most beautiful woman in the world. I remember being so proud because of her beauty and poise. When she'd come to school for parent-teacher conferences or to pick me up, all the heads would turn. My mom's a great person, not just a beautiful one. She has so much class and treats everyone with kindness. I have always been very proud of that.

I remember thinking that both of my parents were special because of the way they treated people. My father used to say, "Never step on others to get ahead, and treat all people the same." Even though my dad is one of the most famous men in the world, he has always thought of himself as being on the same level as everyone else, no matter what their position in life. So I grew up like that. To me, everybody's the same, even celebrities. When your dad's Muhammad Ali and such a great man for what he stood up for and for being his own person, a man who has had a lot of what he worked for taken away and survived . . . nothing tops that in my book. My dad is Muslim, and there was a real emphasis on religion in our family. We were also taught pride, humility, and confidence and to be thankful for everything that we had. A lot of times people who grow up privileged see the people around them not necessarily treating everybody with kindness and respect. But in my family, that wasn't the case.

As a kid, I always wanted to grow up fast. As a teenager, I couldn't wait to be independent. I wanted to start working. I wanted to move out of the house. Being Muhammad Ali's daughter was a challenge because I didn't always know who my real friends were, and there were always different people around me. I struggled to find my own identity. Sometimes I felt teachers gave me a harder time because they wanted to make it a point not to give me an easier time. I never wanted special treatment, so I tried to keep who my father was from people as long as I could. When I enrolled in school, I used my mom's last name, which was Anderson at the time. That's how much I wanted to be on an even playing field with everybody else.

I never played team sports as a kid. I did well in PE class, but I wasn't interested in team sports. I wish I'd participated in sports earlier on because then I would have discovered that I was an athlete at a younger age. That's why now I tell parents that sometimes you have to make your kids do certain things so they can figure out whether or not they even like them. If you leave it up to them, they'll say, "No, I don't want to do that. I don't like that," without even trying it. Who knows? If I'd just tried when I was younger, I might have done something other than boxing. But, in any case, once I discovered women's boxing, I was hooked.

I was seventeen going on eighteen at the time, and I was visiting my best friend and her father. We were getting ready to watch a Mike Tyson fight, and some women came on before the prefight coverage. I was amazed when I saw them. I didn't know women boxed, and I wasn't prepared for it. As soon as I saw them, I thought, "Oh my God! I can do that!" I got so excited, and my friend said, "Laila, you could do it, too!" And her dad said, "Yeah, right, Laila. Them girls will knock you out!"

because I was a pretty girl, and he was looking at how rough and tough they were. I remember it was Christy Martin who was fighting. I didn't know who she was at the time. All I knew was that she was a tough brawler who was fighting with a bloody face. But still, I was so drawn to it. I just wanted to do it. I immediately responded, and I realized right then and there, "I can do it. I can win."

The seed was planted. I kept thinking about it and also wondering, "What would everybody think, being that I'm Muhammad Ali's daughter?" At that time I had a little business called Laila's Nail Studio, and I had a full clientele. I was in school at Santa Monica College and planning on transferring to USC for business. I was thinking, "How am I just going to start boxing — you know, drop everything and start boxing?" I knew it would take a lot of work and there would be many eyes on me. I knew how big a deal it would be to have Muhammad Ali's daughter boxing. I never really wanted to be a public person. I never wanted to live the kind of life my dad lived.

It took me about a year to finally make the decision to go ahead and do it. I'm a planner, and boxing had never been in the plan. Going to school was the plan. Having my own business was the plan. To think about changing everything I'd been doing threw me off course. It was a hard decision to make, but I ended up following my heart. I stopped worrying about what everybody else was going to think. I didn't get any help. I didn't go to my dad and say, "Dad, what should I do? How should I do this?" My thinking was more like "I'm going to do this on my own, and I'm going to see if I like it. I'm going to see if I have talent." I didn't want to embarrass myself or my family. If I didn't have what it took, then I wasn't going to do it. I found a trainer, and things took off from there. I trained about three hours every day, and I absolutely loved it, which kept me going, because I was also in school and had the nail salon. I went to the gym at the end of the day. I had to get there by eight o'clock, and I was tired, but what gave me energy was looking forward to what I was going to learn and how I could get better. I fell deeply in love with boxing. I'd never ever been as passionate about anything as I was about boxing.

When my mom finally found out I was boxing, she was positive. She didn't say, "Oh great!" but her response was more like "Oh, really? Is that what you want to do?"

But she told me after the fact, after I'd been doing it for a while, that she'd been thinking, "Oh, God, here we go again," because she'd had to sit there through my dad's fights, scared and on edge until the end. But my mom is very spiritual, and she understands that you have to let your kids do what they want to do and support them. She knows that I'm very hardheaded and that I was going to do it regardless, so she supported me. My dad found out through people I was training with, and I knew he didn't like it. When we had our first conversation about it, he was kind of quiet. He said, "So what are you going to do if you get in the ring and you get knocked in your head and you're dizzy and you don't know where you are? What are you going to do if you get knocked down and you're on the canvas and people are judging you?" Indirectly, he said everything he could possibly say to try to talk me out of it, but I told him, "I'm going to do the same thing you did. I'm going to get up and keep fighting." I felt like no matter what happened, I was going to be able to handle it and deal with it.

I won all of my fights—twenty-four in total, and twenty-one of them were knock-outs. My first fight was in October of 1999, and I remember feeling good but at the same time disappointed that it ended so soon. The girl just wasn't a good opponent, and I didn't know what to expect from her. Most fighters are just happy to win, but I wanted more of a competitive fight after all my hard work and training. My manager at the time told me, "You won. That's all that matters." My response was "Yes, but I wanted to do a little more."

My most memorable fight was against Jackie Frazier, Joe Frazier's daughter. We fought eight two-minute rounds. We weren't fighting for a championship, but we both wanted to win so badly. We had our fans there, which is another thing I liked about the fight, because usually it was just me that everyone was cheering for and nobody would know who the other girl was. But people knew Jackie Frazier, and you had your Frazier fans and your Ali fans. The energy was great, and Jackie was a tough girl. I had the flu before the fight, so by the third round, I was exhausted and ready to fall out. I was expecting to have been done with her by then. It was a good fight, and in hindsight, I wish we'd had a rematch. At the time, I didn't want one because I was adamant about

fighting girls with championship belts, and she didn't have one. But if I'd fought her a second time, I would have been able to stop her instead of just winning, and we would have made some good money, too. But at the time, I just wanted to prove that I was serious and not just Muhammad Ali's daughter, a girl trying to ride off her dad's name.

When thinking about my strengths as a boxer, the first thing I have to mention is my confidence, which I get from my dad. Confidence can take you far in life, especially when it comes to boxing, but it's not confidence alone. You have to have what it takes to go with it. I have confidence plus technically well-rounded skills: a good jab, strong movement in the ring, and an evil streak. For instance, I'm going to try to stop you. I'm not trying to go the distance. Before the fight, I'm going to tell you, "You're going to get knocked out. This is not going to go to the judges." Some people consider this talking smack, but I'm just telling the truth about what I came to do, and you can be sure that I believe every word of it. There was no chance that I was not going to win—ever. It was about getting in there and performing the way I wanted to perform. It's just like with a basketball player, only he says, "I want to run the court this way and make this basket from this corner." I didn't just want to win. I wanted to win in a beautiful manner.

I really had my own style. Some people saw similarities between my dad's style and my own in terms of my movement in the ring or my jab, but he was more of a boxer and I was more of a fighter. You have to be supercompetitive, especially in boxing. One person is going to win and the other is going to lose, and for me, losing was not an option. It's not like in basketball and football, where you know you're going to lose sometimes, and that's acceptable. For me it was like "I'm going to stay undefeated." I looked at every opponent like "It's just me and her. She has two hands, I have two hands, and I'm going to come out on top."

A lot of people don't understand my passion for boxing. They say things like "So you really like to box?" And I say, "Yes!" but it's something that can't really be explained. Don't get me wrong: Even though I love to box, I don't encourage others to do it. I wouldn't want my kids to box, and when young girls come up to me and say they want to box, I don't say, "Oh yeah, this is what you do. I'm going to hold your hand

and show you the game." But speaking for myself, I did what I wanted to do and what I love to do. It's a real sport, just like any other, and the beauty of actual boxing is being able to stand directly in front of someone and hit her without her being able to hit you back. You have to calculate how close you can stand exactly on the right angle to make your move. Many people don't realize that boxing is a thinking game.

Most women don't make a lot of money boxing. It's a dangerous sport, and there's not a big audience for it. If you want to box on the side for fun, that's one thing, but trying to make a career out of it wouldn't be my first choice for anyone. I'm always up front with people because a lot of girls think, "Look at Laila Ali. She did this. She did that." It's true, I couldn't have been successful without being a great fighter, but I also couldn't have gotten where I did without my last name. It took the two, and I try to explain that to people. This may sound crazy, but a lot of my fans never saw me box. They just like who I am and the idea that I'm a fighter, that I'm a strong woman. They think it's cool. "Oh, I love Laila Ali," they say, but they have never even seen me fight.

I stopped boxing when it wasn't fulfilling anymore, when I felt like there was nothing left, which was sad in the sense that I wasn't able to fulfill my dreams of having some great fights against some of the top contenders—against the women I felt were the most competitive boxers. Unfortunately, they didn't want to fight me, and I got tired of chasing after them. Still, boxing has opened up a lot of other opportunities for me. There really isn't anyone else out there like me. There are other female fighters, but they don't have my background. I'm not just a boxer, and I'm also not just Muhammad Ali's daughter. I worked very hard to be able to say that. When I went on *Dancing with the Stars*, right after my last fight, it was an opportunity to show people another side of myself. For a while, there was this stigma with being a female boxer. People used to ask me, "How come you don't have a deal with L'Oréal or Revlon?" But those companies weren't calling and offering up anything. They don't want a boxer to represent them. I really had to soften up, and *Dancing with the Stars* was the perfect opportunity. After that, I did *American Gladiators* with Hulk Hogan for two seasons and a show called *Student Body*, which was kind of like a *Biggest Loser* for kids. And then I started having kids of my own, and things kind of slowed down for me professionally.

I have always thought of myself as a nurturing person, as someone who mothers people and looks out for everyone. In fact, my friends call me "Mama Bear." I love being a mom. There's a part of me that just wants to be a housewife, because I want to raise my kids myself. So I'm conflicted when opportunities come up, and I turn down a lot of them to be able to spend time with my family, to be there for them. In terms of my career, my main focus is promoting health and wellness as well as working on licensing and branding. I have my own line of beauty care products. I am also coming out with a line of healthy salad dressings, seasonings, and marinades in 2012, and I hope to expand my company to include clothing and housewares. My products are natural, earth-friendly, and nontoxic, which is very important to me, and they are high quality and affordable.

I'm the president of the Women's Sports Foundation, which is an organization that Billie Jean King started years ago. It has become the go-to place for other girls-in-sports organizations. We uphold Title IX. We aim to empower girls and women through sports and physical activity, and to make sure they're being treated fairly. I'm passionate about young girls being involved in sports, because sports give them confidence. Sports teach discipline and give girls something productive to do with their time, and they foster friendships. Through sports, girls overcome adversity and learn how to stay fit and active. Sports also help to prevent obesity and, indirectly, teen pregnancies.

Whether it's about being a mom, a boxer, or a businessperson, you can learn something from just about everybody. I grew up following the beat of my own drum, and I didn't pay much attention to what others were doing. Now, at this stage in my life, I'm more curious about what inspires other great women. What inspires me is the feeling of accomplishment I get when I succeed at something. I may not always have energy, but the thought of how I will feel when I'm successful and have accomplished the goal I set out to accomplish usually keeps me going. There's nothing like feeling good about something you have done. Also, I'm inspired by making others happy. I'm inspired by people who not only talk the talk but walk the walk, like my parents, who are very real people. I'm very proud that I have been able to accomplish my goals. I set out to do something and I did it. I have always been that type of person—I do what I say I'm going to do, and I am proud of that.

Nicole Avant

Nicole Avant is the U.S. ambassador to the Bahamas. Previously she was vice president of Interior Music Publishing. As ambassador she focuses on five initiatives: education, alternative energy, economic and small-business development, women's empowerment, and raising awareness of the challenges facing people with disabilities.

✷

I was raised in Beverly Hills, California, and my parents still live in the house I grew up in. My parents are competitive, but in a healthy way. When it came to their children, my dad's focus was finance and my mom's was on reading and education. My father was always the first one up in the morning because he couldn't wait to read his *New York Times*, his *Wall Street Journal*, and every other paper that showed up at five A.M. He was all about "You better know how to count, and you better understand the value of money." My mom read to us every night. She was very concerned with education, because I was one of the few African Americans in my school, and historically, high expectations were not placed on African American students. My mother pushed my brother and me to be serious and do our best. When I was at sports camp competitions, she always wanted to know what place I came in and if I'd done my best. Then she'd say, "Get outside and practice" if I wasn't pleased with my results. There was never any "I can't do this" or "I'm not going to try." If I had to give a speech at school, she would make me rehearse it over and over again. At the time, I thought she was crazy, but now, in my position as ambassador to the Bahamas, I have that same habit: I will read the same speech ten times, until it fits me and I'm very comfortable with it.

My dad worked his way up to being a very successful music executive. He grew up under Jim Crow laws and left North Carolina at fifteen. He did whatever it took to succeed. He worked as a waiter, a stock clerk at Macy's, and a doorman at a jazz club. He went on to become the manager of that club, managed various musicians, started his own record labels, and eventually became the chairman of Motown Records. He recognized early on that wealth led to power and a seat at the table politically—and that power meant being able to have dialogues with politicians. Warren Beatty was the first person to take my father to a political event. He was the only black person in the room, and he quickly realized that while lawmakers make decisions for all types of people, all types of people don't have equal access to lawmakers. This new activism became the foundation for a friendship between my father and Senator Ted Kennedy. Since then, my father has supported many political figures.

Our household was very social. My mother is a philanthropist and surrounds herself with people in the arts, so the mix of guests was eclectic and lively. There were always lots of gatherings, parties, and fund-raisers, but the best part was that everybody—from politicians and businesspeople to artists and entertainers—was really great at what they did, whether or not they were famous. I'm fortunate to have been surrounded by people of excellence. At first, I was completely oblivious to their significance. I remember wondering why everyone made such a big deal of my parents' friends. There was Quincy Jones, who is my godfather and, in my opinion, one of the finest composers in music history; Sidney Poitier, whom I consider one of the best actors of all time; Harry Belafonte; and Muhammad Ali. I just didn't get it! One time, I told my teacher that Governor Jerry Brown of California had been over. She responded in disbelief, asking, "Why was the governor at your house?" I answered, "I don't know." She said, "Well, what was he doing there?" I replied, "Just talking to my father." Eventually, these kinds of conversations made me more aware of what certain people did and why they were considered special. I began to wonder what set them apart from everyone else.

I majored in broadcast journalism at California State University, Northridge, which has a wonderful program. At the time, it never occurred to me that I could end up a weather girl in Kentucky! When that became the case, I was quickly put off from the industry and jumped ship. After a stint at A&M Records, where I'd also worked in college, I joined my father's company, which back then was Tabu Records. It was a great time to be in the music business and a great time for black artists. The S.O.S. Band was really hot, as were Alexander O'Neal and Cherrelle, and they were all produced by Jimmy Jam and Terry Lewis for Tabu Records.

In 1998 I decided to pursue my interest in education and went to work for the Neighborhood Academic Initiative at the University of Southern California.

While I was working at the NAI, my mom kept saying to me, "You better learn more about the publishing side of the family business." Later that year, I went to work for Interior Music Publishing, one of my dad's companies. From there I continued to learn the business and to focus on what my dad was doing. He was still very active in politics and was working on John Kerry's presidential campaign. I remember Kerry's stepson, Chris Heinz, coming into the office to talk to my dad about approaching young professionals in order to raise money. I told him, "You know what? I can help you with that. I'm good at that." He and I became friends, and I ended up doing whatever I could for Kerry's campaign.

I love being a part of a team that has the common goal of working for the good of something. I remember being so excited to participate in a political campaign, at least on a fund-raising level, and I wanted to make sure more African Americans became involved. I was passionate about getting young people excited about politics and about hiring interns to go into inner-city schools to generate interest in helping out with the campaign. I did more of this kind of work for President Obama's campaign, but I got the idea from Kerry's campaign. Between the Kerry and Obama campaigns, I helped out former congressman Harold Ford, Jr., who was running for the U.S. Senate. He used to call me his "chairwoman." On every conference call with his fund-raisers, he'd jokingly ask, "Chairwoman, what do you think we should do?" I was so passionate about his campaign that I flew to Tennessee to work for him. I was devastated when he lost. I mean, he lost by such a small number of votes, but it didn't matter. It was just devastating because I knew how hard everyone had worked and how great a senator he would have been. At the same time, his loss fueled me for what came next, which was Obama's presidential campaign.

The irony of it was that I actually did become the finance cochairwoman of Obama's campaign in California. I called Harold and laughed, saying, "See, you called me 'Chairwoman' this whole time, and now I end up actually being a chairwoman for a campaign and I worry that I don't know what I'm doing. I have this title and people are writing about me in the *New York Times.* What if I can't raise the money? What if I can't do it?" And he said, "You'll know exactly what to do. And if you don't, you'll figure it out." Penny Pritzker, Obama's national finance chair, tapped me for the position. When I told her, "I'm not at that level—I just want to do what I want to do at my level," she convinced me. She said, "You *can* do this." In the end, there were five of us working together—four men and myself—and we split up the state.

Throughout the campaign, my focus and my goal were to make sure that the people doing the grassroots work and the people doing the finance work actually worked together, something that doesn't usually happen. Historically, the people in finance are the big boys and girls, and the grassroots folks are "little college students." We didn't play it that way. Each person was extremely important, and I would remind the donors that our college student volunteers were out there sleeping in their cars and then getting up the next morning to knock on doors. There was a momentum that I can't begin to describe. We just knew we were on to something. For me it wasn't about whether we won. Of course, I'm so happy that we won, but I know that even if we hadn't, this campaign would still have been remembered as the best-run campaign in modern politics.

The experience of being so involved in the election was both intensely wonderful and challenging. When it was bad, it was bad. I mean, there were times when we were so low. There were many people who looked at me and said, "You know he's going to lose, and you're going down with him. He doesn't have a chance, and you're going to look stupid. You're wasting your time." I remember one woman said to me, "You're wasting your family's good name on this man who can't win." The more comments like this would hurt me and shock me, however, the more energy I'd get to move forward and the harder I'd fight—especially because our candidate was a black man. I would get so mad, particularly at black men, and ask, "Why are you cutting this man down? If you don't think he should be president, don't vote for him. But don't sit there and get on every news channel and trash him." I hated seeing other people, especially other black people, go against him. I believe in being *for* people and not against them.

So while I was for Obama, I was never against Hillary Clinton. I wished her the best the whole time and then supported her afterward, when she needed it most.

For me, the game changer, in terms of the campaign, was when Obama gave his "Race Speech." I remember calling one of my best friends, Charles Rivkin, my cochair at the time and now the U.S. ambassador to France. I said to him, "Charlie, people will see who they're voting for when he opens his mouth today." Obama hadn't said a word yet, but I just knew he was going to give a heavy speech, and I knew by the time he was done, people would see the core of him. People who were on the fence would see a top-quality man. I knew that if he was to be taken down over this issue, he would go down truthfully and emerge as a winner spiritually. I knew this speech would change everything because now everybody around the world would have the opportunity to see the Obama I knew.

When the campaign was over, I was able to look at myself in the mirror and, for the first time since we started, say, "You know what? Well done." It was a long, hard two and a half years. When I started out, I had to beg people for even five hundred dollars. I had to sell and sell and sell, to the point that I lost my voice. I was most proud that we were a team, Team California: Charles Rivkin, John Roos (current U.S. ambassador to Japan), Jeff Bleich (current U.S. ambassador to Australia), Tony West (now an assistant attorney general in the Department of Justice), and I. We were a team and we helped one another the whole time. None of us took credit on our own. I was most proud of that. We did it together. We stuck to it and we never let up, not even once.

I met my husband, Ted Sarandos, during the campaign, and we began then what has been a great relationship. After the election, I was very excited to be able to sit down for a while and enjoy married life. I remember people asking, "Don't you want to go to Washington?" My immediate response was "Absolutely not. I don't want to be in government at all." And at the time, I really didn't. Then I got asked if I'd like to be an ambassador. I remember the first time the question came up. I laughed and said, "For what? I'm not even . . . I mean, I'm forty-one, not sixty-one! I have a life in California." People kept telling me, "You should be a part of this." I stuck to my guns until everyone started moving to Washington to take on positions in the new administration. To me, that was when things shifted in my head. All of a sudden, it felt like a very bad divorce. It felt like everyone I knew was busy, that we were no longer talking, that I was no longer part of a team. Then my friend Charlie called and set me straight: "Nicole, to be asked to represent the president of the United States and to say no is crazy. I think you're not thinking straight." I said, "Charlie, I'm tired. It's not something I want to do." He said, "It's not about that." Finally my husband chimed in and said, "Nicole, he's the first black president of the United States of America. He wants you to be a diplomat, and you're going to say no? I know you well enough to say you're going to regret it. One day you're going to look back and you're going to regret not having done it." That's when I started thinking about the impact of this one man. For me, it had honestly been enough to help get him into the White House, but then I started looking at his presidency from a historical perspective: This is the first black man to be the leader of the free world. I have a chance to be a part of this amazing chapter in history and to represent him somewhere in the world. I knew it would be challenging, and I knew it would be stressful on my family and my new husband, but I knew it was an unbelievable opportunity.

I was sworn in by Secretary of State Hillary Clinton on September 9, 2009, in Washington, D.C. I'm the first African American female and the second woman ambassador to the Bahamas, and definitely the youngest by far. In fact, I'm one of the youngest women ever to be a U.S. ambassador. In October 2009, Ted and I chartered a plane and touched down in the Bahamas. There was a small crowd lined up to greet me. I looked at my husband, stood up, and went into "Okay, act as if you've done this before" mode. I walked off that plane and was met by the regional security officer, who said, "I'm going to introduce you to your bodyguards. I'm going to introduce you to your driver. You'll never go anywhere on the islands by yourself. You'll never drive a car. You'll never do this. You'll never do that." I remember thinking, "Oh my God, what have I signed up for?" It's been challenging getting used to this new life, but what has gotten me through every day is the fact that I'm representing the first black president of the United States. I'm his personal representative in a tiny part of the world, but I'm *his* personal representative, and that's a big deal.

My role as ambassador is multifaceted. I make sure that the interests of the United States are upheld in the Bahamas and that the policies the State Department and President Obama want to put forth are enacted. Fortunately, the United States has an excellent relationship with the Bahamas. Our two countries think so much alike that our disagreements are few and usually easily resolved. As an ambassador, I'm also responsible for the safety and well-being of any American citizens living, doing business, or vacationing in the Bahamas. I work closely with the Coast Guard, the U.S. Marines, Immigration and Customs Enforcement, Customs and Border Protection, and the Drug Enforcement Administration. We have the fifth-largest DEA office in the world, which is a big deal. When President Obama asked me what has surprised me most about my job, I said, "Who knew I would end up loving law enforcement? It's fantastic!" I have such respect for people in law enforcement and for what they do. I don't think most of us realize the amount of time and resources that go into our safety. Because the Bahamas is only fifty-three miles away from Florida, it acts as a third border, and the country is a very, very important partner to the United States, a fact most people overlook.

One of the most gratifying aspects of my job is the letters I receive from parents. One mother wrote to me, "My daughter has never watched the news before, but now that she knows you're going to be on, she wants to hear what you're talking about. Well, she actually wants to see what you're wearing, but she always ends up listening to what you're talking about! She sees that she could be something great." I remember another woman who came up to me in a store and said, "It's just your image. You don't understand. You don't have to say a word. It's just the fact that you're black and female and in a very powerful role. That speaks volumes to young girls but also to young boys."

When young people ask me about my journey and for advice, I tell them to stay open to the divine. I tell them I didn't strive to be an ambassador, which doesn't mean I wasn't supposed to become one. What it means is that I had to stay open to the divine plan for my life, because one never knows what the future holds. The key is to get yourself into a situation in which you're part of something that's inspiring and motivating to you—and helpful to others. Do what it is that you love doing, but understand that you'll never know for sure where it's going to take you. I tell people I was President Obama's ambassador to Los Angeles. Although I didn't have a title then, I represented him there, too. There's the conventional way to become an ambassador and there's the unconventional way, but in any case, you're going to have to surround yourself with the people who are going to get you there. Start at whatever level you can, and don't think you're too big for whatever it is. There are a lot of people who began in the grass roots, who were not paid a dime for what they did, who are now working in Washington, D.C. They were committed, they were focused, they were driven.

I'm passionate about living life with a purpose. I want to be excited and inspired by what I'm doing. I love the idea of learning how to live my best life, about developing habits I want to continue and being aware of the things I need to drop. I'm very passionate about education, which is a focus in my role as ambassador. When I'm finished in the Bahamas, I'm sure I'll go back into education, because it saddens me that people are throwing away their lives by not recognizing the importance of quality schooling. Young people end up hating themselves and life and hurting others in the process. It's a vicious circle and a terrible crisis.

One of my biggest inspirations has always been Dr. Martin Luther King, Jr. I read through the book *A Testament of Hope: The Essential Writings and Speeches of*

Martin Luther King, Jr. over and over. My parents also inspire me, as do people who, like them, are passionate, authentic, and unconditionally kind. I think there's a big difference between being nice and being kind. Whereas "nice" is variable—you can be nice one day and not nice the next—"kindness" is a constant. Every person I've ever really been inspired by has been authentic. Take, for example, Muhammad Ali. I love that he is who he is. Over the years, he's made people angry sometimes, but he's remained true to himself, and now everyone loves him for it. Quincy Jones inspires me. I remember spending a lot of time with him and being struck by his talent and passion for what he does. I'm inspired by my husband's creativity, and I'm fascinated by his open mind. I love people with great ideas and the chutzpah to see them through despite what anyone else thinks.

I feel so lucky to have a partner in life and a husband who supports me 100 percent. I wouldn't have been able to take on this job and do it the way I've been doing it without him. There are a lot of men who would have said no. But Ted's not one of them. Here he is, trying to run a major U.S. company, and he gets on a plane every other week to be with me. Having his support and having his love is a huge part of what makes my life great. When it comes to my job, I'm so grateful that I said yes to the opportunity. Most people will never get to meet President Obama, and none of us will ever get to meet the millions of African Americans who came before us, people who for hundreds of years worked so hard and helped build America. They prayed and did the right thing. They focused on education and helped others to succeed. They marched for their civil rights and the rights of others and sat in. And while all of this was happening, these men and women were being terrorized on a daily basis. The most important thing to me is that I haven't let my life go to waste. I've said yes because I felt a responsibility to do so. I've been responsible with my life and feel blessed as a result.

Patricia Bath

Patricia Bath, MD, attended Hunter College before receiving her medical degree from Howard University College of Medicine. As a fellow at Columbia University she developed her interest in ophthalmology and later pioneered the worldwide discipline of "community ophthalmology," a volunteer-based program to bring necessary eye care to underserved populations. Dr. Bath cofounded the American Institute for the Prevention of Blindness and holds four patents in the United States.

✳

My father was a strict disciplinarian and was very focused on education. I probably would have wanted to do well in school and go on to college anyway, but it was a requirement in our household. I look back on that as a good thing, as something that today's parents should have for their children. Children need to be mentored more and given more guideposts. My mother was the heart of our family and the emotional anchor. She was extremely kindhearted and loving, and my brother and I worshipped her. She was younger than my father and really ran the household because he was a merchant seaman and away a lot for work. My father was from Trinidad, in the West Indies, and was a pupil of Professor Eric Williams, who later became the first prime minister of Trinidad and Tobago. My father was an exemplary student, and although the Trinidadian education system only went through secondary school at that time, he received what was the equivalent of a college education. He fostered my interest in math, science, and engineering, because those were his favorite subjects.

My father was a leader and a mediator in our Harlem community. Our neighbors in the apartment building in which we lived, on Seventh Avenue and 122nd Street, looked to him to advocate for hot water and heat and better maintenance of our building. He shouldered that responsibility, negotiating with our landlord even though he was away for months at a time. Prior to his career in the U.S. Merchant Marine, he'd aspired to be a motorman, but he was not allowed the opportunity because of his race. I have news clippings of a report that he scored 100 percent on the Interborough Rapid Transit subway motorman exam but was denied the job. He eventually led other minority subway workers to form a union, and the NAACP handled his case, which he won, becoming the first black motorman for the IRT.

My interest in becoming a physician started when I was four or five and doing pretend play. I would always grab the stethoscope. When I was older, I read about Dr. Albert Schweitzer in the newspaper. I was inspired by this amazing man who left Switzerland to go to the Congo and take care of lepers in the jungle. I was moved by his example and realized I wanted to become a doctor and help humanity. I had a lot of encouragement, not only from my family but also from my community in Harlem, which was very vibrant. My father's best friend, Dr. Cecil Marquez, was among my role models. A family physician and fellow immigrant from Trinidad, he delivered both my brother and me. His office was around the corner, and he made house calls. When he visited, he and my dad would share a drink and talk about island things, such as Carnival. There was not a social barrier, even though he was a physician and my father was a motorman. Back then, there was more interaction between the classes than there is today.

By high school, I was on track to become a physician. My chemistry teacher, Dr. Leibowitz, saw a spark and felt I had something great to offer. He encouraged me to apply for a National Science Foundation Fellowship and guided me through the application process. When I was awarded a fellowship, my photo appeared on the front page of the *New York Times*. As an NSF fellow, I got to do research at Harlem Hospital and take classes at Albert Einstein College of Medicine. It was a fantastic experience and one that really solidified not only my interest in science but also the feeling that I could achieve my goal of becoming a physician. As I look back, I realize self-doubt was never in my consciousness. I was too busy trying to achieve to realize that in ten years what

I'd accomplished would be considered a great thing. I was in the moment and simply enjoying what I was doing. It wasn't a sacrifice to study hard; I loved it.

After high school, I went to Hunter College, which offered me a scholarship. When the scholarship committee asked me how much financial assistance I needed, I said that I didn't know but that I would ask my parents. My parents told me they could afford both the tuition and my books, so I went back to the committee and reported that I didn't need anything extra. I look back upon that with today's glasses, which are not rose-colored, and I realize that many people back then must have wondered, "Why didn't you at least ask for something so you'd have money for clothes?" But that just wasn't part of my ethos. In my family, you worked hard and appreciated when you had enough. You wore clothes that were clean and honestly obtained, and they didn't have to be stylish. The whole idea of having wealth just to have wealth was not a part of the Bath family ethos. I attribute that way of thinking to my parents, who were happy and loving and felt good about themselves as they were.

I had a wonderful undergraduate experience at Hunter. Along with three friends, I founded the college's first science newspaper, which was called the *Catalyst.* I was the editor. I made a lot of African American friends through my sorority, Alpha Kappa Alpha. Sorority life was great because it provided a social network as exciting as today's Facebook. After pledging, I was nominated for a leadership position. My sorority sisters told me, "Pat, you need to run for national office." They campaigned for me at the Boule, our biennial celebration. The next thing I knew, I'd been elected Second Supreme Anti-Basileus, which meant I was on the board of directors of the sorority and held the highest national office for the undergraduates in Alpha Kappa Alpha. As Second Supreme Anti-Basileus, I was given the honor of introducing Dr. Martin Luther King, Jr., who was the keynote speaker at the next year's Boule. I was honored to meet him in person and to be able to chat with him privately for a little while. It was the sixties, and there were all kinds of turmoil and politics in terms of who should be the spokesperson for black people. On the one extreme, there was Malcolm X; on the other, there was Martin Luther King, Jr. As an aspiring physician, I was not interested in politics. I was too busy with matters of science and trying to get accepted into medical school. Politically, I was undecided, but after hearing Dr. King speak, I became a disciple. I was struck by his charisma and spirit. As he spoke, one could not help but be captivated by the power, logic, and elegance of his rhetoric. My entire being resonated like a bass drum with the righteous thunder of his words.

I was quite happy to get into medical school at Howard University, where for the first time I had science professors who looked like me. I finished my MD in 1968 and returned to New York to do an internship at Harlem Hospital. I was part of the first wave of interns from Howard University and fellows from Columbia University to roll up their sleeves and give something to the Harlem community. We were an amazing group, about 50 percent African American and 50 percent white. We were also an experiment. It was the sixties, the era of the Vietnam War, the Beatles, rock and roll, and the promise of utopia. Racial justice was no longer just a dream; it was almost a reality. The powers that be at Columbia's medical school had made a decision to send their best and brightest graduates to Harlem Hospital—at least the ones who were willing to go. I went there primarily because I wanted to fulfill a part of my dream, which was to serve the community in which I was raised.

After completing my internship, I did a fellowship in ophthalmology at Columbia, where I first noticed the health care disparities between the African American and white patient populations. I could just scan the waiting room at the Harlem eye clinic and see that more than half the patients had obvious visual impairment or blindness, which was not the case at the Columbia eye clinic. This observation spurred me to do a retrospective epidemiology study, using data from the National Institutes of Health and the National Eye Institute, which corroborated my observations. This study, published in 1978, produced two important findings: First, blindness was twice as prevalent among African Americans as it was among whites, and second, eight times as many African Americans were blinded by glaucoma in comparison to whites. Part of the explanation for this finding is access to ophthalmologic care, but I suspect there may also be genetic or hereditary aspects that have yet to be found. Sadly, the National Eye Institute has not provided the funding to answer this question, and other organizations, including mine, don't have funds to address the problem.

As I look back on discrimination that I've experienced in my career, I have concluded that sex was more of a factor than race. For example, when I objected to having my office at UCLA in the basement, the response was that they didn't know where to put me because I was the first woman. I wasn't the first African American on the faculty. It didn't seem appropriate to the department—and I'm imposing my thoughts on what might have been their thinking—to put me in an office with all the guys. When the situation was ultimately resolved, I was assigned an office with three women grant writers, but at least I wasn't in the basement. I recently had a chat with my former director, Bradley Straatsma (who has been very supportive at critical moments in my career), and we were laughing about the past. I said, "You know, Brad, there was architectural sexism." He said, "Why?" And I said, "We women surgeons had to change in the nurses' dressing room." Back then, they didn't have a separate dressing room for female doctors, because there were so few of them. Now I can look back upon these things and chuckle. You have to keep your eyes on the prize and not get

distracted by the small stuff. You have to stay focused on your goal and not waste time and energy on things unrelated to your goal. That takes a sense of self. It takes being anchored, being confident, and having a strong support system. My support system has been family: the people, our values, and our ancestral legacy.

From the start, my goal has been clear: I've strived for excellence with each and every patient and to achieve the best possible results. To do this has sometimes meant thinking about things a little bit differently or trying to accelerate beyond existing technology. For example, imagine trying to do something as delicate as eye surgery with a cumbersome tool. I imagined a fine, delicate pen instrument that I could use to very precisely etch the exact portion of the cataract that I wanted to remove. I visualized and conceived of an improved device above and beyond what was then available, and in 1981, I invented the Laserphaco Probe, which uses a laser to vaporize cataracts via a tiny insertion into a patient's eye. After the cataract is removed, the vision can be restored by the insertion of a new lens.

One of my greatest moments as an ophthalmologist was in Tunisia, where a woman who'd been blind in both eyes for thirty years regained her vision after I performed surgery on her. It felt like a miracle. The operation was complex—an artificial corneal transplant (called keratoprosthesis) that even if done perfectly can fail. I could not predict the results, because the patient's cornea was so scarred that we could not see the retina. Furthermore, she had no medical records, so we had no idea of her history. I replaced her damaged cornea, and the day after the surgery, we took off her eye patch. First she gasped, and then we all gasped. When we saw that she could see, we brought her son to her, which was such a touching moment to witness. After all that, we got busy and measured her visual acuity with an eye chart. Postsurgery, she was able to read letters on the 20/20 equivalent line, indicating she had 20/20 vision. I experienced quiet ecstasy. This is why you become an ophthalmologist, a surgeon, a servant of humanity. This is why you sacrifice and tirelessly strive to achieve perfection.

I performed this surgery as part of a team of three U.S. experts, each of whom had donated a week of time to the visually disabled in Tunisia. We were working with a group called Orbis, in conjunction with my own organization, the American Institute for the Prevention of Blindness, which I cofounded in 1976. The AIPB was established because of the disproportionate numbers of blind people in third-world countries, where people don't have as much access to eye care. After working in rural parts of Nigeria, I developed "community ophthalmology," in which general health-care workers are trained to do ophthalmologic triage in order to maximize the impact of the few available physicians. When I returned to the United States, I talked to colleagues, one of whom was a Biafran pediatrician who'd been part of the relief effort in the Nigerian-Biafran War. He was a public health expert, and he and I, along with two other doctors, formed the AIPB to help the blind all over the world. During the early years, we interacted with the World Health Organization in hopes of at least eradicating preventable blindness, such as the kind due to lack of vitamin A. For example, in Sudan, children who did not die of famine may become blind from lack of vitamin A. We were in existence and operating during the crisis in Sudan, but our efforts were a mere drop in the bucket. There is still a lot of work that needs to be done.

Since 2005 the AIPB has initiated a program that donates technology to blind children in Africa. These poor children need all the help they can get to achieve their potential. In February, the AIPB sent ten voice-activated computers to a missionary school called St. Oda near Kisumu in Kenya. In a thank-you letter, the school's headmaster told me that now their school was the first for the blind in the country to have "talking computers." Access to these computers and other assisted technology should be a right. Health care should be free. I believe that as a human being, you are entitled to health care. We have a motto: "Eyesight is a basic human right." Our Constitution states that everyone has the right to life, liberty, and the pursuit of happiness, which I believe includes health, because how can you have a right to life if you don't have access to vaccinations, prenatal care, a kidney transplant, cancer medications, or AIDS medications? It's tragic that health care has become so politicized.

I constantly wonder why all the other nonprofit organizations that have been in existence, and working in Africa for decades, haven't solved the most basic problems I discovered. However, I'm encouraged that there is a new perspective on serving humanity, exemplified by people such as Bill Gates and Warren Buffett. There's a big message in the fact that they've chosen to form their own organizations as opposed to just giving to existing ones. Their conclusions and their observations are mine as well: There's so much that needs to be done. We need new players, and we need new thinking. There needs to be a commitment to utilize the resources and assets that are available and to deliver help to the populations that really need it. I think the problems are fixable. I truly envision a cure for blindness. I hope my legacy in all of this is that I was a tireless and passionate advocate for the blind and that one day the blind will see.

Mary J. Blige

Mary J. Blige is a multiplatinum recording artist and the recipient of nine Grammy Awards and four American Music Awards. She released her first album in 1992 and has followed with seven more through 2009. In 2008 she and Steve Stoute launched the Foundation for the Advancement of Women Now to offer college scholarships and inspire women "to reach their individual potential."

✴

I grew up in Yonkers, New York, in a tough neighborhood. My mother was a single mom who held down at least two jobs and probably three, for all my sister and I knew. She definitely was a hard worker and a real survivor. A fiery woman, she was smart and strong, and she raised us the best way she could. Some of my strongest memories from childhood are of her singing around the house. She could sing so beautifully, and I mean she could sing anyone's songs. And I used to look at her and think, "Oh my God, she's so pretty."

My mom and my sister were my support system when I was growing up. They were the only safe things I knew. In our neighborhood, people were getting held up at gunpoint and killed all around us. It was terrible. There were people who tried to set up recreational programs, but the community was so bad that things would get shut down before they ever really got going. A lot of people around me didn't know how to act. And it wasn't just black people. There were Spanish people struggling, and there were poor white people having a difficult time. Everybody was just trying to survive, and it was awful. I don't really have anything good to say about my neighborhood growing up, except that my mom sustained and motivated me. As a child, I wanted to protect her, and I never wanted anything to happen to her. I believed that if I could stay alive, she would be all right.

Music was always an outlet for me, even as a young child. When I was five years old, Stevie Wonder, and especially *Songs in the Key of Life*, was on regular rotation in my house, along with Rose Royce. My mom would play those records over and over again. Music always helped me. Singing along was so uplifting. I think I realized I had talent for the first time when I was seven years old. Ms. Sweeney, my music teacher, would always pick me for the lead roles in the school plays and talent shows, and she would make me sing in class. I remember thinking, "Ms. Sweeney likes me." I began to realize what she saw in me after I sang in one of the talent shows. I performed "Reunited," which is a male-female duet. While I was onstage singing, I had this aha moment. It felt like "Oh my God, I'm singing his *and* her parts, and I sound good doing it!" I wish someone had recorded that performance. The audience was looking at me as I was singing, and they were real quiet at first, like they were seeing a ghost. Then when the song was over, they just cheered and went crazy. I remember that moment like it was yesterday. I remember them looking at me with expressions that said, "You gotta be shitting me. She's doing both parts and she's only seven!"

I felt so happy because I was getting attention. When you're a child and getting attention, you think, "Yeah, I'm doing something." I felt like I was loved. I knew then that I really wanted to make singing a career. At first I didn't think something like that could ever happen for me, but soon people all over my neighborhood knew I could sing. I had a reputation. People would say, "Mary could sing this song. Mary could sing that song just like that person." It was like there was this force in my neighborhood. When I walked outside my house, people would say, "Yo! Sing, Mary! Sing this!" I took my first turn toward becoming a professional when I went to the Galleria Mall, where they had a karaoke machine. Everybody was telling me I should go there and sing, so I did. I sang "Caught Up in the Rapture," by Anita Baker. I brought the tape home, and my mother's boyfriend at the time took the tape to Jeff Redd, who was already a star, and his people gave it to Andre Harrell. A couple of weeks later, they told me Andre wanted to come to my house to hear me sing. I was thinking, "Yeah, right. That's so far-fetched." I mean, it was like Berry Gordy wanting to come to your house during the days of Motown. Andre Harrell was huge. Andre Harrell was Guy, Jodeci, and Heavy D and the Boyz. At the time, all that stuff was popping. It was the music everybody was dancing to in the clubs. All that R&B, all that Good Guy music, all that good New Jack Swing, all that good Heavy D hip-hop—that was Andre Harrell. Andre was it.

I will never forget when he actually showed up at my house. He was in a black shirt with white polka dots, and he was driving a black BMW. He came inside, and he had on those glasses of his. I sang "No One in the World" and "Been So Long" for him because Anita Baker was my girl. He looked at me like he could not believe my voice, and maybe a year and a half later, in 1989, he signed me to Uptown. I remember being so happy after I got my first deal, and so relieved. I mean, I was so damaged from my environment and from watching my mother suffer so much. I was so relieved because my goal was to get my mom and my family out of the projects. We'd suffered so many horrible nights and days living in that place. I told my mom, "We're getting out of here!" and she was so happy and excited and proud of me.

I attribute my staying power in this business to my faith in God, to remaining humble, and to knowing that without Him providing what I need, I wouldn't be here. I also understand that my fans consistently support me in every single thing I do. I try to give them what they need, and they support me back. I have a responsibility to them as a result. Once you have so many people watching you and listening to you and learning from you and loving you and adoring you and supporting you, you have to think about them. I have to think about these kids. I have to think about everything I represent to them.

It's really important to know who you are, and to know in your gut what's going to work and what's not going to work for you. When you know who you are, you know what clothes you can wear. When you know who you are, you know what deals you can make. Sometimes you end up doing something because you think it's cool or something you could get away with doing, and then you find out you were wrong. Trial and error is what causes you to stay true to yourself: When you step out of you, you can find out what doesn't work for you or isn't you. And sometimes when you step out, you find

something truer. You realize, "There it is. That's what I do. That's who I am." My fans are smart, so when I do something that doesn't feel good to me, I know it's not going to feel good to them either. And that's what keeps me true to myself.

My fans are my biggest motivation. Every time I meet someone who's really a Mary J. Blige follower, I'm so humbled and overwhelmed that I can't even give myself the credit. I believe that it's God working through me when I'm told, "You saved my life," "You saved my marriage," or "Oh my God, Mary, keep doing what you're doing. Please don't stop." Sometimes these comments have come on the heels of naysayers or people who want to push me off to put up the next thing, and I've been thinking, "Damn, are they right?" And then my fans say, "Hell no! We see you! We need you. What would we do without you?" And I'm thinking, "Well, what would I do without you?" It freaks me out when someone like Suzy Welch, the extraordinary author of *10-10-10*, says "No More Drama" is the song that helped her get through her horrible divorce. And then there was the little girl whose face was mangled by a dog. She had to have surgery to be able to speak again, and she didn't feel good about herself. Her mom told me that when "No More Drama" came on the radio after the surgery, her daughter said, "I want to live." Those were the first words she'd spoken in a very long time. These kinds of stories remind me that this thing that I do is really bigger than me. It's bigger than the music. It's a full movement of women everywhere, not just African American women.

The first thing I tell young ladies is to believe in themselves and to work on finding out who they are. I know this is easier said than done, and it's a lifelong undertaking, but start searching, start understanding who you are and everything you want to be. Once you begin to know, you'll be able to access things. You need to believe in yourself first. Believe that God is real. Believe that you are worthy. Oprah has said, "You are worthy because you're here." On her final show, she said, "You are worthy because you were born." That was all I needed to hear, because it's one of the things that has triggered me, too, that has put a cherry on top of everything I was already feeling. It's a feeling like "Okay, I have something to say no matter what, just because I'm here."

One of the reasons I started the Foundation for the Advancement of Women Now was to help women who deserve second chances, women who don't have the money to go to college but want to complete their education, women who want to better themselves. FFAWN provides resources to these women to help them rise. We've already sent twenty-five women to college on four-year scholarships, and we're planning to send more. The Mary J. Blige Center for Women in Yonkers has a GED program and provides child care, because I remember it was hard for my mom to get a babysitter when she needed to work. I think of all the things that hold women back and how the center can address them. There's a computer room where women can get their résumés together or do whatever they need to do to handle their business. I really want the center to help build up women. It's about lifting the spirits of women and helping them to be able to hold up their heads, because there's nothing worse than feeling badly about yourself.

It's important to follow your gut in life. It's probably among the most important things a person can do, because I believe that God is our "gut" telling us what is right and what isn't. I guarantee when all is said and done, you will wish you had listened to your gut more—whether in business deals or in personal relationships. You already know what's real: What's real is what's inside you. One of the best pieces of advice anyone has ever given me came from Chaka Khan, who told me, "Get out of your own way, Mary." I'll never forget that. When her words finally clicked in my head, I awakened. Chaka gave me the same advice about my vocal cords. She said, "When you get out of your own way and you open your mouth and sing, you're going to be all right." And now my vocals are free. At some point I lost my voice because I was smoking cigarettes, drinking alcohol, and doing drugs. I lost it, and I was really messed up. Then by the grace of God, I was healed and my voice is back. My voice is back, and it's bigger because I'm not afraid of trying to do new things, to reach for more. I was no longer comfortable with the norm, and once you acknowledge that you're not comfortable with the norm, you can give so much to so many people and you can give yourself the best life ever.

I feel amazing right now because I'm not being held back by myself. So often we hold ourselves back because we're afraid of what people are going to think. If there's something in life that you need to step out and do or find out about, and your gut is not tugging on you, if it's only fear that's holding you back, then just do it. We hold ourselves back from so many things. We hold ourselves back from love because of what someone else did, because someone hurt us in the past and we're afraid of it happening again with a new person. My current state of mind about life is good because I know what comes with it. It's not all "Oh, every day I'm just so happy!" I mean, I know that as soon as I walk out my door, or sometime next week or beyond, something is going to go wrong. Life is like that, and the beauty of it is that being able to accept that fact is what makes life good.

I'm in a good place in my head. I feel very confident. I feel like I can do whatever I want to do, and I've never felt like this before. I think my confidence comes from who and what I am, which is still developing. I know what I'm not, and I know what I cannot do, so that doesn't bother me anymore. But I think I can do anything I choose to do. And I just believe the best right now. I have to believe in the best because there's so much of the negative out in the world, but that's not where I'm choosing to go. If you can think positive, you will get positive.

Majora Carter

Majora Carter founded Sustainable South Bronx in 2001 to advocate for the development of the Hunts Point Riverside Park and restore the Bronx River waterfront. She founded the Majora Carter Group, a "green" economic consulting group, in 2008.

✳

I grew up in the South Bronx, in Hunts Point. I was the youngest of ten kids. Although only six of us lived at home, my mother took care of neighborhood children whose parents worked, so I was always surrounded by lots of other kids. Education was a really big deal for us, as was having a routine. I assumed that everyone else was raised with the same sort of structure, but I soon realized that wasn't the case. For instance, my mother wouldn't allow me to eat cafeteria food. She made me come home from school, which was only a few blocks away, for lunch. I would eat her food and then go back for recess. Being a little girl, I was upset by this because I never got to experience the cafeteria culture I desperately wanted to be a part of. At the time, I found it annoying, but now I'm grateful for it in terms of the type of food that I got to eat and what I learned to consider normal. My mother knew exactly how much time it took for me to walk home, so there was no messing around after school. When I got home, I would change into my play clothes, have a snack, do my homework, and only then could I go outside. This was understood, and it never occurred to me that it could be any other way. There was a time for work and there was a time for play, and this is a habit that has stuck with me.

As I was growing up, my neighborhood was literally burning around me. It was a time of financial disinvestment, a period in which some landlords actually torched their own property to collect insurance money. The summer before I turned eight, the two buildings on either end of my block were burned down. People that I'd known all of my life, all eight years of it, were suddenly gone. Overnight they were out of the neighborhood. Then, at the very end of that same summer, in late August, my brother was killed in a drug war. Violence was also something that happened a lot.

Obviously, I realized these crazy things didn't happen everywhere, and I never considered them normal. What I did consider normal, however, was the sense of community I felt despite what was happening around me. The fact that my mother took care of other people's children instilled in me a sense of responsibility for others. Our house was a safe space for a lot of people who didn't have the means to support themselves without help, and that was what I understood a community to be about. That was normal for me—the idea that a community looks out for you, even when things are screwed up around you. I'll never forget the outpouring of support we got from people in our neighborhood when my brother was killed. Yes, he was an incredibly popular and beautiful young man, but the support extended way beyond his death. It went far deeper than that, something I'll never forget in any way, shape, or form. People were like, "This is the Carter family. They have been here for all of us, and we're going to be there for them." People don't always get that about communities like the South Bronx. For all the horrible stuff that goes on here, we still want the same things. We hurt the same way, and we, too, strive for lives that are safe, happy, and healthy.

One of my earliest role models was my first-grade teacher. Although she probably wasn't even five feet tall, she was a tower of a woman to me. She helped me to see that I had so much to offer the world, when I didn't believe that I did—because I was a little black girl. Years later, when I was admitted into the Bronx High School of Science, a specialized school that has produced a great number of Nobel laureates, I knew I had some chops. I truly believed I could be something great in this world, though at the ripe old age of fourteen, I wasn't sure how I was going to do it.

I remember one of the young people my mom helped to raise. He grew up, went away to college, and became a lawyer, and he did all this cool stuff. One day, he brought over his girlfriend to meet my parents. She was a director of photography for a soap opera, and she'd won an Emmy. She was this beautiful, fabulous black woman, and I thought, "Oh my God, I want to grow up to be just like her." I remember sitting at the kitchen table and watching her talk. She was utterly animated and totally sure of herself. She knew she had a place in the world and a place in society, and she was going to live out loud, regardless of what anyone said a black woman could or couldn't do. I remember writing in my journal that night that I'd met the person I wanted to be when I grew up. We have since become friends, which is funny and wonderful.

I went to college thinking I was going to major in theater, but I soon realized I didn't like being in front of crowds. I not only found I preferred production and design, but I also discovered that I really wanted more saying power. Eventually, I moved into film, which I could use as a medium to tell the stories that mattered to me. When I graduated and started working—and I use that term loosely—in the film industry in New York City, I probably made less than a thousand dollars over the course of a year. I couldn't support myself and had to move back in with my parents, which was not at all fine with me at the time.

In moving back home, however, I got involved with the Point Community Development Corporation, which was working on youth development and community revitalization in Hunts Point. I wanted to use the arts as a strategy toward revitalization, so I ran a film series and a film festival with a competition that turned out to be very successful. We also did some public art projects and, completely by accident, got involved in some environmental work when I found out that the city and state were planning to build a huge solid-waste transfer facility right on our waterfront, a facility that would be used to process 40 percent of the city's garbage. The proposed site was eight blocks away from our center, so we were compelled to do something about it. In 2001 I founded Sustainable South Bronx, through which we aggressively and successfully lobbied for a much more sustainable solid-waste management plan, one that didn't completely discriminate against a poor community of color the way the original one did. With the founding of SSBx, I developed the first waterfront park for the neighborhood in more than sixty years and created one of the nation's first green-collar job training and placement systems, which to this day is still the most successful. I also raised the profile of sustainable development in poor communities of all colors around this country.

Two of my earliest mentors were Yolanda Garcia and Leslie Low. Yolanda was part of a group called Nos Quedamos, which means "we stay" in Spanish. They fought the city's urban renewal project, which was basically code for "We're not going to ask you what you want. We're going to come into your community and drop a plan on you and move you out and then do whatever we want with your neighborhood." Nos Quedamos fought the city's plan and submitted their own instead. I couldn't believe what they were able to accomplish. Yolanda encouraged me to speak from the heart and to talk about what I know. She was so kind and gentle, yet at the same time she had enormous expectations. She would say to me, "Majora, you're a leader. You cannot decide that you're too shy to speak on behalf of your community when it needs you." When I said, "I don't like talking in front of people," she replied, "That has nothing to do with anything. Nothing." Her belief in me gave me the strength I thought I lacked.

Leslie Low, who ran the New York City Environmental Justice Alliance at the time, said similar things to me. She encouraged me to see myself as a leader, which I didn't by any stretch of the imagination. To be honest, I think up until a few years ago, I cringed when I heard people refer to me that way. Part of it was a lack of self-esteem—women can be really goofy that way. We're taught to put ourselves in the backseat, to not make waves.

I was in a social therapy group for many years. Honestly, I went because I wanted to get over some stupid guy who'd broken my heart. But over the course of time, I realized I was being held back by my attraction to the kind of men who reinforced all the horrible things I thought I was supposed to believe about myself—that I wasn't very smart and that I had nothing to offer the world on my own. One of the women in the group had been an incredible political activist for most of her life, and she helped me to realize that what I thought of as a liability—being born poor, female, and black—not only made me see, feel, and interpret things in a unique and valuable way, but it also led me to act on them in ways that a lot of other people might not. I came to understand that this insight could be used to help and support others. Though I'd been a part of—and, in many cases, spearheaded—a lot of good stuff, I hadn't given myself credit for it. When I thought about it more, I realized, "I did it! Yeah, I did." The shift in how I saw myself and my accomplishments was slow to happen. Believe me, at first I felt like I was performing or, worse, lying to myself. But later on I was able to recognize and acknowledge my accomplishments—something I had always been reluctant to do.

I left Sustainable South Bronx in 2008, which wasn't a hard decision to make. The tendency for burnout in the world of social justice is incredibly high. I'd reached the point where the stress and the attention I was getting were dragging me down. I'd won a MacArthur Foundation Fellowship and was internationally known, yet I had to hustle speaking engagements to pay the bills. By the time I left, a third of my agency's budget was generated by speaking engagements, not by foundations, and that wasn't sustainable for me. It was taking me away from the work I loved. At the same time, I couldn't help but notice as I traveled around the country that my talks drew the craziest crowds. It wasn't just community activists who were coming to hear me speak; it was architects, people from the business community, and city officials. It was a wide cross section of people, yet I hadn't changed my message for anybody.

The message I was putting out there, the type of sustainable development I was pitching, clearly resonated with people outside the South Bronx and with many different types of stakeholders. Starting my company, the Majora Carter Group, was a way to help other communities around the country unlock their own local economic potential. Our approach was all about saving money. For example, if you train people in a community to do the type of entry-level environmental service work that a municipality needs—whether it's stormwater management, air-quality control, green roofing, wetland restoration, or urban forestry management—and if you use that as an opportunity to support the community, the green economy benefits everyone. The city saves money because people are working. They're not taking up social service dollars or, worse, heading into jail. They're not receiving unemployment benefits, and they're part of the tax base as opposed to the tax burden.

Currently, we're entering the realm of urban agriculture and working on a plan to develop a national brand of urban-grown produce. The trend has been toward smaller endeavors, such as community gardens, which are wonderful but don't generate substantial amounts of food or create jobs. We envision urban greenhouse centers that use hydroponic techniques to grow ten times the amount of produce that would be possible in the equivalent space through more traditional means. This food supply can be used to augment what is generated by regional growers, ensuring a dependable supply of locally grown produce that can be sold to local metropolitan institutions and retail establishments. We see this plan as a means to create jobs more than as a means to build community, even though we believe that in building a city's economic base, you are actually doing community building in a major way.

It probably sounds clichéd, but I love speaking to young people because in so many ways they are smarter than their elders. When I talk to them, I say, "The generations before yours have made all sorts of really screwed-up mistakes, but you can learn from them and do something different because you know you can. I'm expecting you to do things that I never thought were possible. My expectations of what you can do go way beyond anything I've done." Inevitably, they look at me like, "Okay, you've got to be kidding. There's just no way *we* can do *that*." Yet they have already expressed interest by even showing up to hear me speak. I encourage them to build on what I have done but not to think of that as an end in and of itself.

I try to remind people that we're all connected. When you do something as simple as flush your toilet, it impacts somebody somewhere. Just because you can't see the effects doesn't mean they aren't there. Most people don't want to know that their actions directly contribute to somebody else's pain. I speak from experience. I mean, the people who lived in Manhattan had no clue that when they flushed their toilets or threw away their garbage, they were choking a neighborhood in the South Bronx. Some people didn't care, but I believe that for the most part, people just didn't know. Part of our job was to make everyone realize that 95 percent of New York City's waste was handled by three communities of color. Why would you want three communities handling all that stuff when ultimately, at some level, you're going to have to pay for having done that? You're paying for the public health crisis in those neighborhoods. You're paying for inefficient waste management. You're paying for somebody else's suffering, and you're paying for the lack of innovation. I mean, wouldn't you rather know that your tax dollars are paying for something that supports you, your well-being, and the environment and that is not discriminating against a community of people who are politically vulnerable? Most people would say let's do something different, and that's what was exciting.

I'm most proud of making a link between poverty alleviation and environmental remediation through the development of our green-collar job training and place-ment system. We showed that you can actually save money and resources by having people create and do different types of environmental services that support the communities in which they live and improve our environment as well. I'm passionate about getting jobs for our most expensive citizens—the people traditionally left out of most major economic booms: people who are generationally impoverished, soldiers returning from our oil wars, and the folks who are in and out of our criminal justice system. When you reduce the civil service dollars that go to them, by getting them  gainfully employed, then you have not only a whole lot of cost savings, but you also create a level of dignity for people who have been told time and time again that they don't contribute anything. We have been wasting untold time, energy, money, and resources—not the least of which is the value that people can bring to the table in terms of making our society a better one.

At the end of the day, I'm a black woman from humble beginnings who decided she had a voice and wanted to use it. I do local development strategy. My core mission is to help people realize that they are the keys to their own recovery. It's not going to be

big government or big business that comes in to save you. When people in local communities collectively start to understand that what they have together is something that could really create the kind of environmental, economic, and social change they all want, things get really interesting. It's not all about "thinking global and acting local." When you make smart local decisions, the global will take care of itself.

Debra Martin Chase

Debra Martin Chase became a prolific Hollywood producer after practicing law and working at Columbia Pictures. She set up her own production company, Martin Chase Productions, in 2000 and has produced the movies The Princess Diaries, The Sisterhood of the Traveling Pants, *and* The Cheetah Girls, *among many others, and is currently producing a remake of the 1976 film* Sparkle.

*

Growing up, I was extremely close to my grandmother. She was an inspiration and a motivation, and she was essential in forming my values. When she was thirteen, she moved with her family from New Orleans to Chicago, part of the Great Migration of African Americans from the South to the North. I think she was able to complete only eighth or ninth grade, so her mantra was always "Education, education, education." It was all about education in my family, whether it had to do with opera or literature or other subjects. It's funny, but I have a family that's very close in one sense yet in another goes their separate ways. In any case, we've all realized that we're carrying the baton forward, and that we have an obligation to my grandmother to keep it moving along.

When I was six, my family moved to California, where I attended an almost all-white public elementary school. There was like one black kid in each grade. Always a top student, I was in a gifted program, which meant that I went from elementary school through high school with the same group of kids. I was aware that I was different at many levels, but I still wanted to hang out with everyone in my school, so I was always trying to figure out how to bridge the gaps—both socially and academically. I think many kids, for a variety of reasons, feel that they're different, and that, too, was among my challenges. I felt I had my own space, but as time went on, I found more and more people who shared that space.

I watched a lot of television growing up, and I saw a lot of movies. In our household we didn't talk about politics at the table; we talked about movies. We talked about what we liked and what we didn't like; we talked about the stars. My dad is the biggest movie buff I know and is really the reason I'm in the movie business. I mean, he's seen every movie ever made! To this day, if I have a movie trivia question, I'll call him and he'll know the answer. He likes the classics and the old stars—Clark Gable, Gary Cooper, Joan Crawford, Bette Davis. To him, the golden era of Hollywood remains the golden era.

When I was a kid, I loved *Mary Poppins*. I'd put on the record and dance around the room, singing. I knew all the words to all the songs. Needless to say, when I produced *The Princess Diaries* with Julie Andrews, it was like, "Pinch me." At the end of the day, we all have the power to do whatever we want to do if we believe in ourselves. Most of my movies are about just that, about ordinary women who are confronted with extraordinary circumstances and rise to do what they need to do. My films are empowering and have to do with wish fulfillment. And that's what I tell young women: Whatever you put your mind to, you can do. You have to take the bull by the horns and shape your own destiny. You have to work at it. Things won't necessarily come easily, but if you want them badly enough, and if you're willing to put in the time and effort—if you have faith—you can make miracles happen.

My story is an example. I got into the movie business after graduating from the Harvard Law School and practicing law for about five years. I was working really hard in a big law firm, dealing with big corporations, and I was unhappy. I'd known going in to the job that it would not be a lifelong pursuit. I'd gotten married right out of law school, and finally, at the end of the marriage, I asked myself, "What do you want to do with the rest of your life anyway?"

I'd always been interested in the movie business, but I didn't know anybody—I had no idea how to break in. So at a certain point, I just decided that this was the moment and that I was going to try to do it. I was in New York, and I spent a year

studying the industry because I didn't understand how it worked or what I wanted to do within it. I read everything I could read. I talked to anybody who would talk to me—just to ask questions and make relationships. I went to seminars. At the end of that year, I knew that I wanted to be a studio executive or a producer because they're the people who come up with the ideas for movies, the people who shape and create them. When I first started interviewing for jobs, everyone was like, "What do you know about the movie business? You're a lawyer. How could you do *this*?" I just kept saying to myself, "If somebody's doing this, why can't it be me?"

Eventually, I got my break. While still a lawyer, I attended an executive program luncheon at Columbia Pictures and sat next to Frank Price, who'd just come on board as the new chairman of Columbia, which he'd run before. At the end of the meal he said, "I have this project. It's this book that's set at Harvard. I'd love to hear your thoughts about it." That was on a Thursday. Over the weekend, I locked myself in my apartment, read the book twice, and made notes. On Monday morning, I called him up and said, "I had a chance to read your book. I'd love to talk to you about it." He was like, "Great." So I went up to talk to him. He was interested in what I had to say, we kept corresponding, and then he brought me on as his executive assistant, a job that usually goes to a white guy. I mean, that's like a fair-haired-boy position!

For the next year, I went with him to all of his meetings, I read for him, I helped him stay on top of the issues, and I was one of his troubleshooters. We would sit in his office at the end of each day, and I would ask questions: "Why are you marketing it this way?" "Why didn't you buy this?" "Why are you casting it this way?" I could ask him anything I wanted to ask, and he would answer. He wanted me to learn. At the end of the year, there was a big coup, and he was ousted from the studio. In tears, I ran into his office and asked, "So where are we going now?" And he said, "I adore you, but I'm not taking you with me, because you need to stay here and get a real studio credential under your belt." He gave me a two-year contract and officially put me on the creative staff at Columbia. Meeting Frank Price was my big break, but I got it because *I* decided that I wanted to change the course of my life.

At the end of the day, it was faith—and I mean faith in the universal sense—along with family and friends. I've worked hard, but I've also been extremely fortunate and had a lot of support. In some senses, ignorance was bliss for me, because when I set out to get into the movie business, I had no idea what a unique thing that would be for a black woman. Even though twenty years ago—and I've been in the movie business for twenty years now—there weren't a lot of black partners in law firms, and black women were still working their way up, there was definitely an African American presence. When I finally got to Hollywood, I realized that you could count on one hand the number of black women who were solidly in the business off-camera.

Over the years, I've learned how to put some separation between myself and the business because there's always going to be rejection. There's always going to be stuff that doesn't go the way you want it to go. By definition, the industry's a roller coaster, and in the early years, I was right in there, riding the ups and downs personally: If I was up, I was way up, and if I was down, I was way down. Gradually, I've learned to look at things more objectively. I've learned to take a more philosophical approach.

Though there have been times when I've pushed, pushed, pushed, I've learned that things happen when they're supposed to happen. It goes back to the Serenity Prayer: "God, grant me the serenity to accept the things I cannot change; courage to change the things I can; and wisdom to know the difference." I'm a fighter, and when I make up my mind to do something, I go all out to get it done. Yet experience has taught me that you've got to pick your battles—and you've got to decide if it's even worth going to the mat, because sometimes going to the mat is a waste of time.

Paying it forward is extremely important to me. There have been so many people who have given of themselves to me—so many people who have been instrumental in my life. I feel the desire and an obligation to do the same for others. I believe in karma: I think we're here, at least in part, to make the world a better place. If I can help others fulfill their dreams and be in a position to contribute, then on the karma chart, I get points, too.

In life, there's always the road not taken, and no matter what, you make sacrifices along the way. But the past is not the future, and I'd prefer to think of life as constantly

evolving. Rather than focus on things that didn't happen or decisions that I may regret having made, I focus on making choices going forward that will move me toward a place in which I'm satisfied and happy. Life is not perfect. There are always going to be things that could be better, but you have to continue to work at it no matter what. You have to assess things along the way. It used to be that I'd come off a movie and immediately be on to the next thing. Well, sometimes what's next should be nothing, because I need to reenergize myself, reinvigorate my motivation, gather inspiration.

For many years now, I've been doing at least one movie a year, and that's a big deal, particularly in this economic climate. Disney has been incredibly supportive of me. I've had my company there for more than ten years, at a time when studio deals for independent producers are few and far between. It just doesn't happen. On New Year's Eve, my dad called and said, "Lifetime's showing the two *Sisterhood* movies. That's their New Year's Eve programming." I think he goes through *TV Guide* each week and marks which of my movies are coming on. Recently, there was one weekend when the Disney Channel was running *The Cheetah Girls*, *The Princess Diaries* was on ABC Family, *Just Wright* was on On Demand, and *Sisterhood* and *Courage Under Fire* were on movie channels as well. I must say it was pretty satisfying.

I don't have kids of my own, but I have a splendid group of godchildren, nephews, and a niece. They're very important to me, and I love seeing them evolve and grow up. I've discovered a lot of people and helped them in the movie business — Shonda Rhimes, Anne Hathaway, Blake Lively, Chris Pine, Lucy Hale, and Jesse Williams — and I take great pleasure in that as well. I think part of it is that I like to surround myself with special people — people who help me be the best that I can be in the most positive way.

I'm most passionate about living life to the fullest, about being motivated and inspired. There will always be times I have to reassess what I'm doing and why I'm doing it, but in the end it's about having a good life, about trying to live the best, most satisfying, happy, peaceful, and fulfilling life possible — on a daily basis.

Misty Copeland

Misty Copeland is a dancer with American Ballet Theatre, which she joined in 2000. She became a soloist with the company in 2007. She started her dance career as a young teenager and was considered a dance prodigy. While balancing her ABT schedule, she frequently dances with the pop singer and musician Prince.

✳

As a little girl, growing up in San Pedro, California, I was always attracted to movement, even before I'd ever taken a dance class. My mom had trained in ballet, jazz, and tap. She was never a professional dancer, but she cheered professionally for the Kansas City Chiefs. When my older sister and I were about five and six years old, she would choreograph dance numbers for us, to songs like "Please Mr. Postman." I must have inherited some of her abilities. I was always moving around my house, which was funny because the only form of dance I'd seen was on MTV, and that wasn't the kind of stuff I was composing. I'd choreograph what was natural to my body, which was a more lyrical type of movement—something I'd never seen or experienced before. I used to make my poor little sister, Lindsey, learn the steps. She wasn't a dancer and had no desire to become one, but I needed to see what I was creating. I remember in fifth or sixth grade, I choreographed a dance for two girlfriends, which I forced them to perform at a talent show.

I decided at the end of sixth grade to try out for the drill team. I was determined to make it and auditioned for the captain position, even though I didn't have drill team experience, and had to choreograph my own audition dance. The coach, who was also a history teacher in my middle school, used to tell me that I had the build of a ballet dancer. I didn't know what the build of a ballet dancer was, besides being thin, but in fact, there are exact proportions that schools and companies look for in the body of a ballerina. The coach, who'd danced her whole life, suggested I start taking ballet classes and introduced me to my first teacher, Cynthia Bradley. I was thrilled to have made the drill team as captain, but I ended up dropping out about halfway through the year because of my growing commitment to ballet.

The first classes I took were at the Boys and Girls Club, which was a place that I hung out every day anyway. It was kind of like, "Sure. I'll do this class since I'm already here." I used to show up in sweats and a T-shirt. I didn't like ballet at first. It was a huge change because it required so much discipline. I'd played sports, but I hadn't been on a real team or done such a structured physical activity before. In the beginning, I thought it was almost too uptight, and I probably would have quit if it wasn't for Cynthia. She kept writing letters to my mother and finally called to convince her to let me train more regularly. She kept telling my mom, "Misty's really gifted." Cynthia believed that I had the potential to be a great ballerina. After a few weeks, when we started training more intensely, she said to me, "I don't understand how you know how to hold your head, your chin. You're a natural." She put me in pointe shoes after a couple of months of training, which is rare in ballet. Being en pointe can be dangerous if you haven't developed the correct muscles and technique to hold yourself in the right position, but she felt I was ready. The experience of going en pointe for the first time and preparing for my first big performance were the two things that made me fall in love with ballet. The first time I performed onstage, in front of a big audience, I had no stage fright at all, no nervousness. I felt completely comfortable.

Soon all of my time was taken up with ballet. I'd go directly to the dance studio from school, and I was there every day from three o'clock in the afternoon until about eight o'clock at night. I was taking several classes a day. Since most dancers start dancing when they're about three or four years old, I had a lot of catching up to do. Physically, my body adapted quickly, but the mental aspects, the terminology, came more slowly. I had trouble remembering the names of the steps. It's not just about learning the steps; it's also about training your body and your muscles to look a certain way.

That takes years, and there's no way of speeding up the process, even though I was hungry to learn. At first everything was intriguing to me. I wanted to know as much as I could, and the thought of the next performance was thrilling. Performing was my favorite part because I felt really open and free onstage. For the first time in my life, I felt like I belonged.

My mother was very supportive of my interest in ballet. She said, "If this is what you want to do and you really love it, I'm going to be here for you," and that was that. There wasn't ever a question about whether or not I was going to do it, but at the same time, I was completely sheltered about the real world of ballet. When I talk to former teachers and my mom, I find out things I was completely unaware of when they were happening. When I was about fourteen, I was asked by a company in South Dakota to be a guest artist in *The Nutcracker*. My mom told me later that it was a really big deal that I got the lead, because I'm black, something no one had told the company in South Dakota ahead of time. They just figured they'd let the company meet me and see me dance and then decide for themselves if the color of my skin was an issue, something I thought was really insane when I found out years later. When it came to being black, a lot of things were kept from me until I was a professional with American Ballet Theatre. Until then, I really felt there was nothing holding me back. I just worked hard and figured people would see beyond the color of my skin and recognize my talent. When I was fifteen, I took part in a summer intensive program with the San Francisco Ballet, and the director of the school, Lola de Avila, pulled me aside and gave me extra assistance. I soaked up everything, especially by watching the other dancers and how they did things. Next I studied with Diane Lauridsen, who helped me to become technically strong and to keep my movements clean. I also competed in the Spotlight Awards in Los Angeles at the age of fifteen and won. When I was sixteen, I was invited to participate in a summer intensive with American Ballet Theatre. The artistic director of ABT, Kevin McKenzie, was interested in me for the studio company, but my mom insisted that I finish high school before joining. Just the same, I will never forget when Kevin told me that I had a "natural movement quality." That meant so much to me.

I joined American Ballet Theatre when I was nineteen, which was such an honor. Coming from a small town and a small school where I was a big fish, there were things I didn't realize. I never felt like, "Oh my gosh, being at ABT is so overwhelming because everyone's more talented than I am," or anything like that. I held my own, but it was the first time I sensed that talent alone wasn't going to get me where I wanted to go. That took a really long time to get through my head. In professional ballet, there are many factors that come into play. It's not as simple as being thirteen, having the right body type, and getting a full scholarship because you're talented. It probably took me about five years to understand that it takes more than just talent to advance; you have to truly be your own self-promoter. Now I've been with ABT for more than ten years, working with a lot of the same dancers. Even though it's extremely competitive at this level, there's definitely a feeling of camaraderie when you're onstage together. It's an amazing and bonding experience.

I'm proud that after six years I was promoted to soloist at ABT. It was incredibly challenging to be in the corps, which was crushing at times because you don't get much feedback or support. Even though the majority of company ballet dancers don't make it beyond the corps de ballet, I trusted my value. I remember the day I made soloist: It was the end of the 2007 season at the Met. I was hanging out in the dressing room, and I got a call that Kevin wanted to see me. When I got to his office, he began by telling me that he knew it had been a "long, hard journey and now your time has come." In retrospect, I'd describe our conversation as surreal. I'd always envisioned that when it happened, I would throw myself at his feet, crying. Instead, I stood there in shock. Becoming a soloist was a big deal in itself, but the acknowledgment that I had received from the ballet community felt just as important.

I've had amazing female role models in my life. My mom has been the biggest influence. Everything about her is incredible, as a mother and as a person. Susan Fales-Hill is another inspiration. We met because she was on the board of trustees at ABT. She is, first and foremost, an incredibly successful and strong black woman, but she has also been so supportive of me over the years, especially when I was in the corps waiting for the opportunity to become a soloist. It was a frustrating time, and she assured

me, "They're interested in you. You have what it takes." She really helped to pull me out of the occasional funk and to stay on track. With Susan as my sponsor and mentor, I always feel there's someone on my side.

I'm inspired by all the little black girls and boys who send me letters and visit my Facebook fan page to tell me that I'm the reason they dance and how much it means to them that there's a black person who has made it in ballet, that there's someone they can look up to. It's not just about me anymore. I feel a responsibility to them to get as far as I can in the field and to break down as many barriers as possible along the way.

It's hard for young black dancers to think they can make it in a huge way, in one of the top companies, which are predominantly white, when there's no one who has done it before. Having me there inspires them to stay focused on their path. It's easier for young African American dancers to venture into modern dance because our body types and our skin color are more accepted there, but if you love classical ballet, then it's important to have a role model. It's extremely rare to see African American dancers with companies like American Ballet Theatre, the New York City Ballet, the Royal Ballet, or the Paris Opera Ballet. In these huge classical companies, there's never been a black woman who's made it to the top, in part because we've never been given the opportunity. Ballet is such an old art form; it's all about culture and history, and change has come slowly.

After so many years of dancing, I still enjoy getting up in the morning and taking ballet classes to warm up for the day. I enjoy keeping up with my technique. I mean, I never stop learning, and I'll never perfect my art. There will always be more to know. I most enjoy being able to perform, being able to express myself, and being able to inspire people through dance. One of my favorite ballets is *Giselle*—the story, the movement, and the romantic era fit my body well, and it's such a beautiful ballet to watch. In real life, I'm most like Kitri from *Don Quixote* because she's strong and fiery, and I am as well, thanks to my mother and my career.

My current state of mind is one of eagerness. I feel almost the same way I did when I first started dancing—just as excited and hungry. Ballet hasn't grown old for me, and I haven't done nearly everything I want to do. There are so many roles I have yet to dance. My dream is to play Giselle. That's a role that suits me well. It would be amazing to be Odette/Odile in *Swan Lake.* Having a black woman play that role would be groundbreaking. Though I still haven't achieved my biggest goal with ABT, which is to become a principal dancer, my heart keeps pushing me forward. Many people have asked me, "Why don't you just join another, smaller company? Or a black company? Why don't you be an independent artist?" Why? Because my heart won't let me. I can't give up my dream of making it to the top position. Not just for me, but for so many other black dancers.

Ruby Dee

Ruby Dee is an actress known for her work in A Raisin in the Sun *(1961) and* American Gangster *(2007), for which she was nominated for an Academy Award. She is also a well-known civil rights activist and in 2005 was awarded the Lifetime Achievement Freedom Award by the National Civil Rights Museum.*

✳

As a young girl growing up in Harlem, I was inspired by my stepmother, Emma. She, more than anyone else, was responsible for nurturing my early creative impulses. She studied under W. E. B. Du Bois at Atlanta University and later became a teacher. She also wanted to be an actress and had a lifelong love of literature, which she passed on to me. She was constantly telling us about Du Bois, and when we got older, he came to our house and we met him. She used to tell us that if you came late to his class, he didn't even look at the door. He would just point his finger to the door, which meant, "Don't come in." That element of strictness was also in my stepmother—she was very much a disciplinarian. She had four children she didn't give birth to, yet she knew each one of us deeply. Her expectations for each of us were so high. She was able to see something in each of us, and she knew I was going to be an actor. With each one of us, she found and nurtured that thing we were going to do.

I lived in Harlem, and I grew up with extraordinary teachers and friends. There was something about the people who lived around us, all kinds of people. And I could slip into different characters when I was a kid. Even today, I know there is no part of anybody that I can't find in myself. I just have a people passion. It was my stepmother who pointed that out to me, but I didn't realize it until later—that one person is a lot of people.

I am a proud alumna of Harriet Beecher Stowe Junior High School in Harlem. The teachers there worked tirelessly to prepare nine of us for the admissions test for Hunter College High School. Up until then, inner-city children had not had the opportunity to take the entrance exam. But with the advocacy of the PTA, our parents, and those wonderful teachers—who drilled us and grilled us after school—we became the first students from Harlem to attend Hunter High. It's why, whenever I hear disparaging commentary about public education, I cannot keep silent. It made all the difference in my life. It opened my eyes. That's what I love about teachers and parents, and that's the responsibility our educational system has got to understand. And I think about the Creator—I think about God and mothers and fathers and parents and teachers, and they are part of the "becoming process"; that is, the process of what we become. We are a reflection of those people.

From Hunter High I moved on to Hunter College, where I became involved with the American Negro Theater. The ANT, cofounded by Frederick O'Neal and Abram Hill, was established to provide black actors, playwrights, directors, and other theater professionals with opportunities to work in productions that illustrated the diversity of black life. They formed the company in the basement of the local library in Harlem, in what is now the Schomburg Center for Research in Black Culture. It was a small room, with an even smaller stage. There was no backstage to speak of. We literally waited in the wings, up against the wall, to go onstage, because the space was so small. And yet no single experience has shaped my journey as an artist more than those days at the American Negro Theater. Many of us were fortunate enough to move up and out to careers in theater and film—some became very well-known: Sidney Poitier, Harry Belafonte, Hilda Simms, Helen Martin, Clarice Taylor, William Marshall, and Alice Childress, to name a few. It was an extraordinary place to train and perform.

I did not always know I wanted to be an actor, but I decided there are no mistakes in this world. When you have something growing inside you, like acting was within me, there is always something pushing that growth, and you have to listen to it. An oak leaf grows like an oak leaf; it doesn't grow like a peach leaf or any other kind of leaf, and they are all beautiful but incredibly different. It occurred to me that each of these leaves came with a mechanism for eternal life. It came with a mechanism for becoming something else, like dirt that becomes fruit. It doesn't die. Now, I think that's how it is with human beings, too. I can't think of such a concept as "nothing." I can't think of what is "nothing." When you go into the room and say, "There is nothing in the room," that is a mistake. If there were nothing in the room, you couldn't breathe, you couldn't live.

I am most proud that I have been able to affect others' lives in the way that I have, that my presence might have enhanced others' journeys somehow. I first felt that effect while working on *The Ossie Davis & Ruby Dee Story Hour* in the seventies, and then with three seasons of *With Ossie & Ruby* in the eighties on PBS. We read short stories and we had all sorts of guests on our show. We also started reading the writers of the day: John Oliver Killens, Langston Hughes, Zora Neale Hurston, Sterling Brown, and all the writers I learned about from my mother and from Ossie. I am just so passionate about poets and underrepresented writers. People told us later in life that their parents made them listen to us, and a couple even told us that's how they decided to become writers. Ossie was absolutely in love with authors; he himself was one, and he pushed me to become one as well.

My one-woman show, *My One Good Nerve*, began as a book of poems and short stories. Though I had been writing this and that—poetry, children's stories, et cetera—I never really called myself a writer. For a long time, Ossie had said I was a humorist and had encouraged me to focus more on my shared-aloud writing. And it turned out that much of what I had written also lent itself to performance. And I didn't even have to audition for the part.

In 2005, Ossie and I received the Marian Anderson Award for humanitarian leadership by an established artist. Though the ceremony occurred after Ossie passed, we were informed before he left us that we'd be receiving the award. It was during Marian Anderson's famous recital on the steps of the Lincoln Memorial that Ossie, who was in the audience, was so inspired that he vowed to marry art and activism as best he could. So for us to receive an honor in her name was particularly gratifying.

Ossie and I were both very active in the entire Civil Rights Movement and deeply involved with the March on Washington in 1963. In fact, we were the masters of ceremonies at the march. Unbeknownst to many people, Malcolm X secretly attended the march. Contrary to popular belief, Malcolm X and Dr. King were not adversaries. Ossie and I always understood that both men had tremendous respect for each other. They knew they represented two ends of the same burning candle. Malcolm asked us to let Martin know that he and his followers were at the March there to back him up in case things got out of hand.

I am often asked if there is a secret to an enduring marriage. I was married to Ossie for almost sixty years, but I don't believe there was one thing that made us last.

Marriage is a process. Love is an aspiration and hard work. When you get married, you think you love each other, but when you live together on a daily basis, especially for a few years, and you come to know each other, you come to understand that love is a process. Personally, I didn't really know what love was until I had been married for a while and had lived the life of this companionship and learned what it takes to get along with another human being whom you choose to spend your life with. That is the exciting part of love itself. You arrive at love. You may think you know it when you marry, but you discover it when you've been through things and answered questions, come upon obstacles, solved things, and swum the rivers of human affairs as richly as two individuals can. Love is like a magnet, a compass. Though confusion may come, love will draw you back on track. And when you look back, you realize it's a blessing, or if it's not, you will know that, too. And when you have a good, solid partner, that partner is part of that magnet, if you're lucky.

I'm told *The Politics of Love*, a film I did last year, is about to be released. I have two roles in independent films on tap. Meanwhile, I'm still on the road from time to time. Mostly, I'm busy with my writing. I wake up in the morning — or sometimes in the middle of the night — with ideas, some so funny they make me laugh out loud. I'm hoping to get some of those ideas on paper.

Today I am inspired by Oprah Winfrey. She reminds me of a trait I found in my stepmother: They are both people whose visions are grounded in selfless agendas. And I feel that she thinks a lot about her responsibility and tries to make a difference in the world, and not only in her own life. She has done so many things for so many people, and she is such a generous person, which I don't mean merely in a worldly sense, but in a spiritual sense. She is one of the drum majors for justice and divine inspiration.

I used to have regrets, but I've come to not think of things as regrets anymore. Rather, they are lessons that move me someplace else in consciousness. I am working on a piece about what I think the role of today's elder community should be. I call it *The Galloping Grannies*. I think it's a shame to die comfortably in your bed with the world in the shape it's in. We need to get involved as meaningfully as our minds, our circumstances, our consciousness, and our best judgment dictate. As elders, we have walked the walk.

Marian Wright Edelman

*Marian Wright Edelman is a children's rights activist who graduated from
Spelman College and Yale Law School. In 1973, after years working in Washington, D.C., she founded the Children's Defense Fund, which advocates for
poor, minority, and disabled children.*

＊

My childhood in Bennettsville, South Carolina, was filled with rituals and the
safety of family, community, and church. When I was a child, my life was
structured and we had clear values. We knew we would go shopping on
Saturday morning, shine our shoes in the afternoon, and take baths that night. The next
morning, we'd go to church and Sunday school. After church, we'd visit people in the hospital, and later in the day we'd have dinner with the faithful and the good, great cooks in
the church. These family rituals are missing today, as is the predictability of childhood.

Despite the fact that I grew up in a small town that was rigidly segregated, I
was part of a cohesive community in which there were strong ties between family and
school and church. Our public school teachers were our Sunday school teachers and
our Girl Scout leaders. Our community elders—the great women of my town—were
formative. They created a cocoon for children and were buffers against the external
world. Today, many of those buffers have disappeared and left children prey to external cultural messages that teach violence and irresponsible sex and excessive materialism. We didn't have all of those external cultural signals back then because we didn't

have a whole lot of TV and music. In today's world, there are far fewer mediating institutions to counter our culture's eroded values. More than ever, you need to have a family that sits down and has conversations, a family that talks to you about what you saw on TV. Many American families don't sit down and have a meal together in the course of a week. Children don't learn how to set a table because of the absence of socialization. I think about how to weave this lost sense of community and family and church back into our lives, so that all children can get the instructions and the structure and the examples that they need to grow into purposeful adults.

The rituals and structure of childhood have been torn asunder, yet rituals and structure for our children are so important. They socialize children. They teach them values. The habits and examples set by adults convey what's important. When I was a child, family members and valued community elders knew that reading and education were important, that service was important, that community was important, that life was not about you, it was about making the world better. Most people didn't have a whole lot, but they shared what they had. They valued children, and they valued education. I think back on all the folks in my hometown who were not educated and who supported and lived vicariously through my education. I think back on the community's pride whenever I achieved something educationally. Many of today's children are missing that clarity of values. They see adults saying one thing yet doing another. The hypocrisy of adults is a big problem in our culture. I have always felt blessed that my parents were who I thought they were. And they lived—tried to live—what they said they believed. My daddy raised me to believe that I will never lack for cause or purpose, and that understanding has been the guiding principle in my life.

We always had books in our house. We always had the latest literature. My daddy had a book-lined study and would spend hours every day reading and informing himself. He'd read with us in the evenings. All of us Wright children realized that the only time our daddy wouldn't give us a chore was when we were reading! I achieved in school because it was expected of me, and because the importance of education was always stressed. Another thing that was extraordinary about my parents was that they didn't raise their girls differently from their boys. I always knew that I was as smart as my brothers, and I was expected to achieve as much in the outside world as they did. It was always clear that all of us would go to college. The last thing my daddy said to me as I rode with him in an ambulance the night he died was, "Don't let anything get between you and your education."

The combination of the good and the "you don't like the way the world is, you change it" attitude toward the bad of my childhood formed my sense of purpose. My challenges growing up included segregation, discrimination, the poverty all around me, and the loss of classmates to premature death because they didn't have adequate health care. Because we didn't have a swimming pool like the white kids, the black kids swam in the local creek, which I later learned was the hospital sewage outlet. That's where my friend jumped off the bridge, broke his neck, and died an early death. There was always a lot of death and hurt in the external world, and children suffered because of poverty and discrimination. I couldn't stand being excluded from libraries and pools and drugstore counters. I couldn't stand the signs that said WHITE and BLACK. The world belongs to every child. To this day, I can't stand for any child to be excluded from anything.

I'm passionate about justice and fairness for all children and their families. The Children's Defense Fund, which began in 1973, grew out of a parent organization that was started in 1968 as part of Dr. Martin Luther King, Jr.'s Poor People's Campaign. I had moved to Washington, D.C., to help Dr. King prepare position papers for the Poor People's Campaign. After he was assassinated, I stayed in D.C. to help set up the Washington Research Project, a public interest law firm. Five years later, WRP evolved into the Children's Defense Fund because I thought that the country was not at all sympathetic to poor and minority adults and that we should focus on prevention and early intervention. I mean, how can you hold a two-month-old baby accountable for not being deserving?

My journey with the Children's Defense Fund has been one of trying to create a level playing field for all children, regardless of their color, the lottery of their birth, or the parents they didn't choose. My life is based on service and trying to build a better country for the next generation. The whole foundation of the American Dream and the

Civil Rights Movement was the parents who sacrificed everything. These parents had few resources but wanted their children to have a better education and to be able to do better than they did. I look back at a lot of the children who were in the Birmingham Children's March, who got hit with fire hoses and cattle prods in Mississippi, who encountered daily harassment, who watched their families be shot at or pushed off their farms, and I'm just amazed. I'm amazed at their courage and extremely grateful that I have had the chance to know these great role models. I have always felt lucky

to be who I am, living in the time I do, with the convergence of great historical events, great people, and great leaders. I mean, to have known Benjamin Mays, Howard Thurman, Mordecai Johnson, Martin Luther King, Jr., Fannie Lou Hamer, and countless great people who have had enormous grit—what a wealth of experience. I want to share as much of that experience as I can, because children need to know that they can change things and to know about the people who did change things. If we don't know our own history, we're in danger of repeating it, of going backward—as we're at risk of doing now.

The greatest national security problem that our country faces today is the fact that we're not investing in our children—in the future generation. Our greatest challenge is that we have a public school system that is failing 60 percent of all children. These students cannot read or compute at grade level in fourth, eighth, or twelfth grade. More than 80 percent of black and Latino children cannot read or do math at grade level in fourth, eighth, or twelfth grade. Forty percent have dropped out of school. A child drops out of school every eleven seconds. These children are being sentenced to social and economic death, and these minority children, who are facing a more than 80 percent failure rate, are going to be the majority of our child population by 2019. Our failure to prepare our children to be our future workforce and to compete with Chinese, Indian, Japanese, and European children is going to be our nation's undoing.

Racism and racial disparities are still very much alive. The two driving forces behind the "cradle-to-prison pipeline" are racism and poverty. Blacks are disproportionately poor and Latinos are disproportionately poor, and the poverty rates have grown worse. Seventy percent of black babies are born into single-parent households, to mothers who have never been married and are among the poorest people in the nation. Imagine your chances if your mother is a poor teenager with no education! We have come to rely on punishment as a first rather than last resort. We have got to change that paradigm. We have got to emphasize prevention and early intervention. We're faced head-on with the fact that the majority of our children are going to be non-white children, and we have to decide whether we're going to keep jailing them—or letting them kill each other, or have guns everywhere, or drugs everywhere—or make them productive citizens. Another big issue is the absence of adult voices to challenge the many racist policies. I mean, CDF talks until we're hoarse, but the black community does not stand up when a five- or six-year-old child is arrested on school grounds. What in the world is the matter with us?

Though we can't predict what the job appreciation will be, the unemployment rate for a black male who is under thirty and hasn't finished high school is currently 43 percent. Literacy is absolutely critical. This is our future workforce, and it has to be able to compete in the global marketplace. If we're writing off a majority of that workforce, it is and will continue to be a disaster. If you can't read, you can't get a decent job. I mean, you can't even read a set of instructions. That means you're going to go into the underground economy. In significant part, that is what is fueling the high incarceration rates.

The United States is the world's biggest jailer. We're spending three times more per person for prison than for public school. Many of the folks we put in prison have dropped out of school. In fact, there is a high correlation between prison, the inability to read, the failure to finish high school, and unemployment. And then when prisoners come out, they can't get a job. They are politically disempowered. This cradle-to-prison pipeline is undermining the social and economic progress of the last fifty years. It's bleeding the hope out of our community, and its impact is growing bigger all the time. All of us are affected one way or another by crime. As a society, we spend hundreds of billions of dollars on dropouts—on people who could be a productive part of a vibrant economy. Incarceration is not only costly, it leaves us less safe. New York State has been spending on average about $210,000 for each child in the juvenile detention system. These young people have been placed in secure facilities upstate, which are simply job creation programs for the largely white counties in which they're located. Most of these children are black and brown. It's the dumbest investment policy in the world. Seventy-five percent of the children in prison are there for nonviolent offenses. When they come out, even though they've been in there for nonviolent offenses, they're angry, and the recidivism rate is about 80 percent. Too many of these facilities are simply creating criminals who would never have been criminals had we kept them in school, had we developed community-based treatment programs that are a lot less costly. We adults have lost our minds, expelling or arresting children at younger and younger ages. Six-, seven-, and eight-year-old children in New York and all over the country are being arrested for things that used to be handled in the principal's office. We're criminalizing children rather than educating them, which gets back to the importance of dealing with the whole child.

The Children's Defense Fund is countering this problem in a direct, hands-on way through CDF Freedom Schools, which are integrated summer literacy programs. Achievement gaps are caused by poor schooling in public schools, but they are also caused by summer learning loss. Many middle-class and upper-class parents send their kids to camps and other enrichment activities, but parents of poor children usually don't have that option. Reading is a cornerstone of our program. We pick the very best books in the world, the theme of which is "Our children can make a difference in their lives, in themselves, in their families, communities, school, nation, world." Our children learn to see themselves in these books. They see their lives and their problems, but they also see hope.

Across the country, children in our Freedom Schools are taught by college students. Our children are getting better test scores because they've gotten into learning. They experience the joys of reading and see the possibilities that open up as a result. Freedom Schools are a two-generation empowerment and leadership training program. We've had about ninety thousand students, kindergarten through twelfth grade, go through the program, taught by nine thousand college students. Each year about fourteen hundred college students, mostly black and Latino (between a third and a half are black males), train intensively at the Alex Haley Farm, our leadership training base, for more than a week before delivering the Freedom School curriculum to about ten thousand children in eighty cities in twenty-eight or so states across the country.

One of our goals now is to get a Freedom School on every black college campus, so that children can see college—instead of prison—in their future. You can't see what you can't imagine, what you haven't been exposed to. Each child learns about what children did in the Civil Rights Movement, that children are not citizens in waiting. Our students have lobbied for their own health care and learned in the process that they can be engaged citizens. They've participated in service activities because we want to try and cement the idea that education is for giving back. We want children to be able to contribute to the community.

In Washington we work on policy and focus on Title I of the Elementary and Secondary Education Act, which is the largest federal program for supposedly equalizing education funding at the federal level. Education funding is still not equal, so we spend a lot of time trying to establish a formula that more fairly allocates money to rich and poor districts and to rich and poor children. The system still isn't fair, but we are lobbying mightily. We're trying to make sure that the accountability provisions that give us good data and the ability, at the federal level, to close achievement gaps are maintained, because there has been an effort to eradicate them. We're trying to make sure that children in the juvenile justice and child welfare systems are treated fairly and get targeted services. We're trying to put into place full-day kindergarten. The entire federal blueprint for education reform by the Obama administration, which we support, is K through twelve, yet only eleven states have full-day kindergarten. If you're building on the assumption that kids need kindergarten in order to graduate from high school, then you need to make sure the kindergarten step is a strong one. The last piece of it is to put into place an early childhood support system, because our high school graduation rates don't start in high school—or even in elementary school. You must reach children from birth to make sure every one of them has access to a high-quality Head Start program. We were successful in getting the right to home visits built into the health reform law, but Head Start reaches only 50 percent of the children who qualify for it. We'd like a high-quality universal pre-K system and a high-quality universal K system so that every child is ready to learn—and every school is ready to help that child learn.

How you can help is to open your eyes and see what is happening to the children in your community. There is no excuse for convenient ignorance. There are uninsured children all around you. There are uneducated children all around you. There are children who need permanent homes. If between 10 and 20 percent of the churches or faith congregations in this country decided they would find foster or adoptive parents for these children, we could clean out the child welfare system. If the judges in the juvenile courts knew there were institutions in the community—a sorority or fraternity, a congregation, or a civic organization—to which they could refer children, to keep them out of the secure detention facilities, we could divert many of these children to more positive places. If there were tutoring programs and Freedom Schools everywhere, children would begin to get an alternative vision of their future. They could learn how to read. They could see kids who are going to college. All this money we spend on entertainment, on cars, on shoes—we could tithe 10 percent of that to lift up the children who are poor and give them hope, to support our institutions, or to target a gift to every black college. Those of us who went to historically black colleges can encourage our alma maters to sponsor and partner with Freedom Schools.

No one has an excuse not to do something. Each one of us should get out there, be informed, and vote. Every year we tell people how their representatives in Congress voted for children. We hold them accountable. You should know your congressperson's record when it comes to cutting or protecting children's programs. For God's sake, get out there and get involved in this budget fray and make sure that they do not tear down the safety net that took so long to build up, that they don't ravage Medicaid, ravage the children's health insurance program, or ravage Head Start or child welfare services. That's all a part of what the budget debate during the summer of 2011 was about. We have got to be involved in the process and let our leaders know you don't cut the poor in order to enrich the rich more. You don't cut children in order to enrich the powerful. We need to be engaged in this debate. We have got to reclaim our children. We have got to rebuild our families. We have got to turn off the TV and pick up books and encourage our young people to pick up books and start book clubs. It's called "voice and vote."

There's not a day that I don't think about my parents, who were my greatest shapers. But the two folks I wear around my neck are Harriet Tubman and Sojourner Truth, who had undying spirit and a burning desire for justice. They didn't wait for Abraham Lincoln or anybody else to free them, and they saw beyond themselves. These were illiterate yet brilliant women. Harriet Tubman couldn't read a book, but she could read the stars and knew the way to freedom. She had the courage to come back and lead other people there. Sojourner Truth could not stand slavery or any second-class treatment of women, and she was the first slave woman to sue to get back the child who'd been taken from her. Both women stood up and fought, regardless of whether or not they thought they could win. They fought because it was right and just, and because they believed in who they were and what they stood for. Their example inspires me and keeps me going.

Whoopi Goldberg

Whoopi Goldberg is an actress and comedian. She is one of the few perform-ers who have won an Emmy, Grammy, Academy, and Tony Award. She is a cohost of the daytime talk show The View.

✳

My mom is a big hero of mine. When I think back on my childhood, I remem-ber I always knew that I was safe. I had a mother who could beat up Drac-ula if he showed up—and it doesn't get any badder than that! She always told my brother and me that we had the right to be who we were, regardless of what other people thought. We always thought this was kind of cool and progressive. We were really lucky to have our mom. My brother and I talk about it all the time. The three of us—my mom, my brother, and I—we're a strange bunch. We're singular and we're quiet. I know this sounds kind of crazy when it comes to me, but it's true.

My New York City neighborhood growing up was totally multicultural. We lived in Chelsea, in the projects, where you learned a little bit of every language because, more often than not, your friends' parents were immigrants. To get by, you had to be able to speak a smattering of whatever language they spoke. You wanted to at least be able to say, "May I use the bathroom?" or "You look very nice today."

We didn't have many family rituals as I was growing up, but in the summertime my mother would take us out to Coney Island, or if we were really good, we could go to Freedom Land, which was kind of a strange, wonderful place that was like a cow-boy world where you could go on rides. But one of the things I remember most was, no matter what, my mom always made Christmastime special. I mean, first there would be a tree. Then, a couple of days later, you'd wake up and the tree was sort of decorated.

Then a couple of more days would go by, and the windows were washed and stenciled with pictures. More ornaments were added, and now there was tinsel on the tree. Of course, by Christmas Eve, it was totally done, and there were decorations everywhere. In the middle of the night, you'd wake up to the smell of turkey cooking, and you'd get up because you thought you were slick. You'd look out of your room, and there still wasn't anything under the tree. But when you woke up on Christmas morning, boom! There were bicycles and books, trains, and all kinds of wild stuff. It was a lot of fun, and I could never figure out where my mother had hidden everything. My brother thought she gave it to the neighbors to hold, but if she'd done that, how come their kids didn't find it?

I'm dyslexic, which, when I was a child, was an odd thing. No one was freaked out by it, but it was difficult to explain because no one knew what it was, either. There was no word for dyslexia when I was a kid. Everyone just thought I was slow. I never gave it much thought. I just knew what I could do: If you told me something, I could remember it. If you showed it to me, I could remember it. If I had to read it, it was more difficult because the words moved around. And, you know, in the olden days, when you said stuff like that, people thought you were crazy: "The letters are moving." "No, they're not." But my mom was different. She was like, "Well, whatever's going on, I know you're not doing it on purpose, so we'll see what we can do." She would read to me, and I never felt that I wasn't smart or equal. I just knew I was different: I did things differently. I thought things differently. My mother's attitude was that I didn't have to go any faster than I could go. She believed in me no matter what.

I would say my first big break came when Mike Nichols saw me perform my one-woman production, *The Spook Show*, and decided to put me on Broadway. I remember when we were in rehearsals for *Whoopi Goldberg on Broadway*, and I was walking down the street with Nan Leonard, the publicist for the show. She turned to me and said, "You realize this is probably the last day you're going to be able to do this this way?" I said, "What do you mean?" She said, "Well, once tomorrow hits . . . I'm just telling you, things are about to change rapidly." I said, "Well, maybe they'll think I was terrible." She said, "No. I can tell you it's gonna get different." And she was right. The next day, we got a wonderful review from Mel Gussow in the *New York Times* and everybody knew me. They knew my picture, they knew what I looked like, and they knew I was doing a show. All of a sudden, people were just glad to see me. It was kind of great. Next, we made a show for HBO, and then I went on to do *The Color Purple*. Over a relatively short period of time, because of a series of breaks, I emerged as a performing artist, someone people were beginning to recognize.

These days I don't know that I'd still call myself a performing artist. I'm more of a monologist now. I have this monologue that I do. Some of it's funny, and some of it isn't. It's like a thought process that lasts for an hour and ten minutes.

Everything inspires me now. Everything makes me happy. Everything that I think I need to be doing, that I am doing, makes me happy. I feel like the world is my oyster. I think I can do anything. What makes me get out of bed in the morning is the fact that I have a job at a time when a lot of people don't. I think my greatest achievements to date are having fairly good relationships with my family and with the people who come to see me perform—that and being a decent person. Those are the biggest boosts for me.

My current state of mind is peaceful. I have nothing to prove and no one to prove it to. I say what I mean, and sometimes I mean what I say—unless there's a better way to say or do it, in which case I'll evolve. I'll say, "Okay, I see this is better than what I had in my head, so we're good." I try to correct things when I think they're wrong. I'm not afraid of doing that. And I'm not afraid of being misunderstood. If someone is willing to ask me what I mean by what I'm saying, I'll explain.

As I said before, my mom is a big hero of mine. Her attitude was "You never have to go any faster than you can go," and that sentiment has had a lifelong impact on me. Nelson Mandela, John F. Kennedy, Jr., Richard Pryor, Moms Mabley, Elizabeth Taylor, and Shakespeare are all heroes of mine as well. They were all individuals. That's the thing: Each of us is unlike anyone else who came before us. We're all originals. I think I can do anything. And I like that.

When I first got famous, people were sort of accepting, but also they were waiting for me to fail, calling me a flash in the pan. I wanted to show folks that I wasn't a

flash in the pan, and longevity is the only way to do that. Time goes by, you wake up one day, and you realize, "I'm still here. Where are they?" That's when you know you're okay. The best advice anyone has given me on this journey is to have a good time no matter what. Enjoy yourself. Enjoy your life, and don't wake up to discover that you haven't had time to have fun.

Thelma Golden

Thelma Golden is the director and chief curator of the Studio Museum in Harlem. She is a lifelong New Yorker and graduated from Smith College. Previously she was a curator at the Whitney Museum of American Art, where she was known for her support of emerging artists.

✴

My parents were both born and raised in New York—my father in Harlem and my mother in Bedford-Stuyvesant, a neighborhood in Brooklyn. I grew up in St. Albans, Queens, in a three-story detached house with a driveway, a backyard, and a front yard. My parents spoke a lot about issues of race and empowerment and about what it meant to own your own home. Our home was located in a community that was predominantly African American. People in our neighborhood were committed to making sure the aspirations of everyone who lived there were supported. My mother was an incredibly creative woman who thought deeply about how she could make a positive impact on her environment and valued the power of aesthetics. My father was an entrepreneur. He was an insurance broker with his own business. Many of his clients were also entrepreneurs. He would take us to meet them, and we would see that, literally, the husband, the wife, and the entire family were working together, that their effort was a family affair.

Growing up in New York, I was surrounded by complexities that were a result of the diversity of the city in terms of culture, race, ethnicity, and religion, but at the same time I was sheltered in some ways from the intensity of it, because I lived in the world that my parents carefully created for me. My parents provided a base of security and an amazing sense of being loved, and our multigenerational, tight-knit extended family ensured I never felt alone or insecure in the world. There was always someone around me—always someone to take care of me. I have three aunts on my mother's side, each one with a distinct personality. My mother saw her relationship with her sisters as defining. In turn, each of them influenced me in her own way, which my mother encouraged.

My mother's greatest gift to me was that she recognized early on that I was my own person. My obsessive interest in culture was not something that she necessarily shared day to day, but she supported it just the same. When I was a child, the Museum of Modern Art was my Disney World. Whereas other thirteen-year-old girls fought to wear lip gloss, I fought to take the subway into Manhattan to be able to go to a museum or performance by myself—and she respected that, even if it caused the occasional struggle typical of adolescence.

I was what people would call a precocious child. My father read the *New York Times* every morning, and by ten years old, I did, too. From an early age, my sense of what I wanted to do and who I wanted to be was formed by the *Times* critics and what they had to say. I'd read about the Merce Cunningham Dance Company, Alvin Ailey American Dance Theater, or the New York City Ballet and think, "I want to see that." I loved *Live from Lincoln Center* and other public television programs featuring theater and the performing arts. By the time I was twelve, I was also as deeply into literature: Toni Morrison, Alice Walker, Toni Cade Bambara, and Gayl Jones. I'd already read *Jane Eyre* and *Wuthering Heights*, both of which I loved, and had moved on to African American literature. I was always small and, as a child, looked younger than my age. If I was told, "I'm sorry. You're too young to take out this book from the library," I would make a big fuss, be the "little girl with the mouth." My parents were supportive of me in any case and understood my need to learn and explore my interests.

I was fortunate to be able to attend an amazing independent school on Long Island with a great curriculum and wonderful arts programs. Though I liked to make things and enjoyed the creative process, I really fell in love with art history. I saw works of art that filled me with wonder and awe, and I knew that they stemmed from a talent I didn't possess. I recognized the power of great art, whatever the form—written, musical, or visual—to transport me to a different time and place. I knew I could learn more about myself and the world through art. I was drawn to the work of African

American artists — literary artists, theater artists, visual artists — because they showed me profound and powerful ideas about my culture. Through African American literature, particularly by women, I began to understand how others would understand me. I went through my teenage years with a romantic sense that I could construct a persona through my engagement with literature. Toni Morrison's *Sula*, the story of an unbounded woman who lives two lives — the one that was given to her and the one she creates for herself — was transformative. For me, Morrison's words introduced the possibility of personal invention.

In high school I began to imagine my life and my future place in the world. I recognized there'd be a day when I'd move out, go to college, make decisions on my own, and get a job. In many ways Vern Oliver, the head of my high school, was the person who made me understand the importance of creating a life that was satisfying and gratifying through a commitment to ideas that are larger than oneself. My freshman or sophomore year in high school, she gave me a vintage copy of Ralph Ellison's *Invisible Man*. People have asked me, "What moment changed your life?" Well, that was the moment. *Invisible Man* was a passport to my future: I would be involved with culture — African American culture, in particular — artists, and amazing creative visions. I would be informed and inspired by the power of creativity. That novel set my path. In many ways Ms. Oliver, through that gift and its impact on me, led me to my course of study in college, where I double-majored in history and African American studies, and to the Studio Museum in Harlem, where I first worked as an intern.

I've had significant role models along the way, people like Lowery Sims, who broke many different barriers in her role as the first African American curator at the Metropolitan Museum of Art. A pioneer, Lowery was at the forefront of the cultural community. I knew of her work all through my high school and college years, and then I had the great privilege of working with her, and she was a beacon of all that I hoped to achieve. There was also Lisa Phillips, my colleague at the Whitney Museum of American Art and a curator deeply involved in identifying the newest and most innovative work. As a curator, Lisa realized my dream of working with living artists. As a child I remember seeing a picture of Mary Boone sitting at the Odeon with Julian

Schnabel, Robert Longo, and David Salle. Years later, in 1994, I was at the Odeon with Gary Simmons and Lorna Simpson, thinking, "Okay, this is what I'd hoped it would and could be."

I'm passionate about art because through the experience of it, we're given the opportunity to better understand ourselves, our history, and this moment in time. Art also gives us the opportunity to better understand those who occupied our planet before us and how they expressed themselves creatively. What made me come to work at the Studio Museum in Harlem was the simple fact that if it hadn't existed, I would have been compelled to create it. What makes me stay is that it deeply reflects my

personal passion and vision. The best part about being at the Studio Museum in Harlem is that I'm helping to preserve and promote an important historic legacy while also supporting living artists. Our mission includes an involvement with the past and the collection and presentation of works of art, but as our name suggests, the artists' studios within the building are integral to the mission of the institution. Artists work here, and that in and of itself is vital. The institution does not only look backward, it looks forward. Directly involved in supporting the work of the present, it is actively ensuring the work of the future.

Although I don't have a checklist per se of what makes something a work of art, I ultimately consider intention first. If someone calls something they've made art, I'm willing to respect that it is art. However, my criteria for what makes it good or interesting art are more subjective and complex: Is it important? Is it significant? Is it interesting and innovative? Does it reflect the intention of its maker? Those are the kinds of questions I ask. I certainly don't have expertise in all periods or kinds of art, but I can say that I know intuitively when I'm in the presence of a masterpiece, whether it's something I've studied or not. When I'm in the Asian art wing at the Met, and I see those very small and delicate Chinese porcelain pieces, I know in my heart that they're great works of art. I can tell that the artists who made them had clear intentions. I can see that the skill and the patience that went into them are not things that could just be learned, that they had to come from a place of deep passion.

My greatest achievement is that I've been open to the many extraordinary possibilities that have been presented to me. Along the way, there have been skeptics, those who didn't necessarily see the value in the vision I had for myself, even before I could articulate, "I want to be a curator. I want to work in a museum." The idea that I was going to live deep in the nexus of important creative production did not sound like a job to some people. Perhaps it seemed like I wanted to be sitting in the South of France with James Baldwin, sipping a cognac while Miles Davis was playing and Judith Jamison was dancing (which is indeed a worthy fantasy). But what I was really saying was, "I don't know how I'm going to do this, but I want to work in an organization that is promoting and presenting culture."

Contemporary African American artists are the deep beneficiaries of the hard work and struggles of the defining midcentury generation: Romare Bearden, Norman Lewis, Elizabeth Catlett, Charles White, Jacob Lawrence, Charles Alston, Alma Thomas, and others. These artists, and the transformative work of the curators and art historians of their era, forced acknowledgment of the need for a change in the art historical canon. Their efforts led to the creation of institutions like the Studio Museum in Harlem and to fundamental changes in other institutions, which finally understood that they, too, needed to better represent the breadth and depth of American artists—not just African Americans, but Hispanic Americans, Asian Americans, and women as well. We're at a point in history when African American artists in particular, and artists of African descent in general, are acknowledged around the world. They're present in museum collections and in exhibitions. Best and most important of all, however, they're present in people's understanding of what constitutes contemporary art—unequivocally and without need for explanation—which is a fantastic, amazing thing. In the words of Frederick Douglass, "If there is no struggle, there is no progress."

Bethann Hardison

In the 1960s, Bethann Hardison modeled for such industry greats as Oscar de la Renta and Calvin Klein, and later on she helped launch Click Models before forming her own modeling agency, Bethann Management.

✳

I grew up very happy in Bedford-Stuyvesant, a neighborhood in Brooklyn. I was an only child and a little spoiled. I loved my mother, who encouraged me to be very independent. From the age of seven, being a latchkey child, I'd walk home alone from school, let myself in, change my clothes, and eat whatever she'd left out for me. I used to meet her at the train station when she'd get off from work. I just loved her style. I loved how everybody in the neighborhood knew her, how everybody talked to her, how all the men liked her. I loved every boyfriend she ever had.

When I was twelve years old, I went to live with my dad, which was a different song and dance. My dad was an Islamic leader, and I was very impressed by him. He was a handsome guy, a smart guy, and very suave. I think the thing that made him strong was his religion, which became my religion. The practice, the dedication, and the discipline I learned from him have stuck with me. He also taught me the power of the individual voice in the face of government. He taught me about writing to the secretary of state, who at that time was John Foster Dulles, to voice my concerns. When I was thirteen or fourteen and the Suez Canal was being invaded, I sent beseeching telegrams. He made me aware I shouldn't believe everything I read. He taught me to keep an eye out for propaganda, no matter how important or powerful the particular source of the information. He taught me to think for myself. These lessons have been very, very valuable to me.

I used to run track for the Police Athletic League in Brooklyn. I was completely committed to it. My incredible coach, Coach Palmer, remains with me in my head. When you've had a great coach, you never forget the things he told you. When I ran relay, I would always look back, and he would say to me, "Never look back. Just run your own race, Bethann. Run your own race. Save the time." Then he'd make me run extra laps! Now I tell kids what he told me: "Learn to run your own race."

When I was in junior high, I chose to go to an all-white high school that black kids were being bused to, instead of the performing arts school I'd also been accepted to. This experience was one of the best things that ever happened to me because I grew very powerful in that school. It gave me a great foundation. I discovered who I was and the freedom to explore and express my ideas. I became the school's first black cheerleader. Each year, the school held something called "Sing," a performance competition among sophomores, juniors, and seniors. It was a musical, like *Glee*. The student body elected the person who would direct and produce the show, and in my junior and senior years, they chose me. I led my class to victory each year I was chosen. These kinds of things happened to me in merging with white kids and liking them; I was easily accepted and as a result got to do things that enriched my life. Through this experience, I learned that if you have the goods and can demonstrate them, if you bring them to the table, you can succeed—no matter who you are or where you come from. It's all about skills and trying, about socializing and being yourself. Sometimes other black kids would say to me, "Oh, you think you're white now," an unfair accusation, but I gained the confidence to handle it as time went on.

There were many things that happened in my high school life that prepared me to work in the Garment District doing what I now realize I was destined to do. As a kid, I hadn't felt that I was yearning for anything in particular, because I didn't dream like other kids. I just followed the yellow brick road. That's the truth of it. The runway modeling thing came about when I was already working in the Garment District. At the time, I was an assistant to Sylvia Courtney at Ruth Manchester Ltd., a junior dress house, and she took me under her wing. I was one of the first black girls to get a job in a showroom. One day, when I took some garments over to Federated Department Stores,

I met Bernie Ozer, who was the head of merchandising for junior dresses and sports-wear. He was getting ready for a fashion show, and on the spur of the moment I said to him, "If you really want to have a great show, you need to put me in it." He immediately said, "Who are you?" I said, "I'm with Ruth Manchester, but if you really want a good show, put me in it." I didn't know anything about runway modeling—nothing. I just knew about entertaining because I'd been a child tap dancer. When I got back to work, Sylvia called me into her office and said, "Bethann, what did you say to Bernie?" I told her the truth but said I hadn't meant anything by it. She said, "That's great, Bethann, but now you're going to do it, because he asked me if you could." I couldn't believe it. I ended up doing the show. The audience had never seen anything like me before. As someone new to showing clothes to an audience as a model, I didn't model like others; I mostly performed. I knew what I was going to do and did it. After that, Bernie kept me on and always used me, and inevitably the crowd would be waiting for me to come out.

Gillis McGill was the first agent to take me on, yet she didn't really like me or understand me, but I was recommended by designer Chuck Howard. I mean, I didn't have a lot of hair, I wasn't the lightest-skinned model, and I worked in a junior area. All of the models who were working regularly at that time worked for the top houses and designers. And those models were much more mature and elegant. I was alternative. I was very dark and very skinny with very, very short hair. I was like the new wave about to come. I mean, I never put on a stitch of makeup, I wasn't girly. In my mind, I wasn't Yves Saint Laurent couture, more Rive Gauche. People like us were on the edge, we thought a whole different way. But McGill took me on and sent me to Bill Blass. He was the fashion industry's Clark Gable. I mean, that's what he looked like, that's how he presented himself—he was up on a pedestal. When I walked into his office, he said to me, "Wow. You're with Gillis McGill?" When I said, "Yes," he said, "I'm going to tell you something. I'm amazed because I would never have imagined that Gillis McGill would take you on." He went on, "Listen, I think you're unique. You're not right for me, but you've got something. But I'm very surprised that Gillis gets it."

If someone didn't specifically ask for me, I never heard from McGill. Fortunately, however, Chester Weinberg requested me out of the blue. He was a very important designer on Seventh Avenue, like Geoffrey Beene and Bill Blass. So Chester booked me for one of his shows, which in those days were held in showrooms, kind of like salons. He sent me out in the first outfit, and I tried to be as elegant and feminine as I could be. People began to whisper, then they got a little louder, and as I went up and down, they got even louder. It was so damaging because it was clear they were talking about me. It was terrible. When I went backstage to get my second outfit, Chester dropped everything and came to help me dress. He said, "Look at me. You're so beautiful. You go back out there." So I went back out there. It was like being in a cage with a lion. The audience wasn't paying any attention to me, so I took on a certain style of walking that was very defiant. When I finished and came back, Chester just held me. Tears were coming down from my eyes, and he wiped them away and said, "It's okay. It's over now and you were great." No one who looked like me had ever done what I'd done before.

In the seventies, I would travel to Europe and model for Issey Miyake, Jean-Charles de Castelbajac, and Claude Montana. My last show was in 1981 in the United States, and then I called it quits. I told myself, "This is the last show." Even if they screamed, "Bethann, do something, Bethann!" If they screamed my name one more time when I walked out, if they wanted me to perform, I still thought, "This is it. I can't. I have nothing more to give." And that *was* it. I'll never forget Polly Mellen, the editor of *Vogue*, saying, "Come on, Bethann! Do it!" I was like, "I'm done. I can't do nothing else." I'd had a great run, but I was ready to walk away from it all, to once again follow the yellow brick road.

I knew I could always get a job because everybody in the fashion world wanted me to work for them. Eventually, I connected with Frances Grill, an agent I knew through my Swedish boyfriend. She'd started this little modeling agency in New York, in the Carnegie Hall building, and she had eight black girls and six white boys, which didn't make any sense to me. In any case, she had me, her son, and this other incredible guy together, and we were the original team of Click Models, which changed the entire industry. It was phenomenal. We went up against the big boys without even trying, like we were positioned by the spirits. Our vision was very different from that of Ford, Wilhelmina, Stewart, and all the other agencies. It was more alternative. The girl

next door wasn't the girl we wanted, but we found the boy next door before anyone else did. We found the volleyball player, the surfer, and the snowboarder from out West. We found the kids out on Long Island, the potato diggers, the clam diggers. We found all those kids, and they were interesting and beautiful. Fashion photographers liked our style because it was different. Calvin Klein, Ralph Lauren, and Perry Ellis were the main clients of the agency, and they loved me and were interested in anything I was a part of. We represented people like Whitney Houston, when she was a young teen. We started Talisa Soto, who was a Calvin Klein girl. Isabella Rossellini was our girl. I got us Tahnee Welch and a girl by the name of Bonnie Berman, a blonde who became a top model. We changed how everything was seen. It was fun, but it was a lot of work.

One night I was at Mick Jagger and Jerry Hall's house, and I was introduced to a lawyer who knew all about me. I was sitting down talking to him, and he said, "Can I talk to you next week, because I hear you're working very hard. Are you an owner of Click?" I'd never even thought about that. I said, "No. What's that got to do with anything?" He said, "Well, how much are they making?" I said, "I don't know." He said, "What's your salary?" So I told him. He said, "Are you happy with that?" I said, "Well,

I feel like if I need something, I can always ask them." He said, "What do they do for you?" I said, "Well, they pay my phone bill and they pay—" He said, "Uh-huh. And you have Click models staying with you from time to time?" I said, "Yeah." He said, "Bethann, I think there's more to you than you think there is." That was the beginning. After I left Mick and Jerry's house that night, new ideas were buzzing in my head.

Not long after meeting that lawyer, a male model friend of mine by the name of Joe McDonald took me for a taxi ride and said, "I want to tell you something about yourself. If you don't learn to walk away and start to do for you, the people around you are not going to be around, and you're not going have the support that you could have. Because, Bethann, you've got to stop working for other people. You're building them, and you're not building you. Everyone knows what you're capable of doing because you keep proving you can do it." I didn't understand any of this stuff at the time, but I did start to think, "What if I . . . ?" That was the key I put in the lock that opened the door to telling myself, "Well, if you don't want to do it for you, then do it for the community you came from. Because obviously you've got something that a lot of people there never had. Here you are, sitting in a white world, doing all the things you've done, and people think you're something. So do it for them."

I had to get some inspiration if I was going to pull this off, because the truth is I felt just fine where I was. I didn't think I wanted to have my own company. What would I want that for? That sounded like a lot of aggravation and no holidays. But both these conversations got me contemplating a change. People kept asking me to come to Paris to meet with them, and finally I said to myself, "I've got to stop ignoring these opportunities. I'm just coasting. I'm being comfortable. There's something I'm ignoring. I'm not being ambitious." Soon after, I went to hear a motivational speaker. He asked the audience, "How many of you feel like when you work, when you're with people, that you don't want to upset them? You'd rather not rock someone else's boat? You'd prefer to just get the job done and not make a disturbance?" I had no problem admitting I was one of those people, so I threw up my hand. A few other people did, too. Then the man looked at us and said, "Then you'll never get anywhere." I knew he was right. It was what I'd needed to hear. At the end of that week, I quit Click. I went in and resigned.

So there I was, out in the world, without a job, without a pot to piss in. I had Bonnie Berman and Talisa Soto, who was all of seventeen at the time, telling me, "You need to have your own agency. We'll do anything for you." They were telling me, "You've got to do this on your own. We've got your back. Don't worry. We'll be there for you. We'll help you. We'll come with you. Just do it." So I began to look for a space, and I started Bethann Management. Though Talisa ended up not coming with me (she was underage and her mother blocked the move, which broke Talisa's heart), she was the one who really pushed. And as for Bonnie, who was the top model in the world at the time, her mother called me out of nowhere and said, "My daughter told me all about you. We're here to make sure you land on your feet. We'll give you money for your bills. Do not let anything fall behind. Your rent, your utilities—anything." Everything fell into place. I found a space on North Moore Street in Tribeca. The lawyer who talked to me at Mick and Jerry's house, his whole law firm stood behind me and charged me nothing. They took care of the negotiations for the space at 36 North Moore—and everything legal related—for nada. Suddenly, my life became Bethann Management. Twenty-one years ago, I started with eight kids and slowly grew. At first I had primarily white kids, with a few brown, Latin, and Asian ones, but soon the group was all mixed. Bethann Management looked how the world looked.

There were a lot of tough moments along the way. I remember that Peter Moore, a Click model, came down to check on me every so often. He'd say, "You okay down here? Your lights still on? Water still running?" He told me what they were saying uptown: "She's not going to make it. How could a black woman with no money make it? She ain't got nothing." I said, "Did they really say that?" He said, "Didn't I just say they said that?" I said, "Okay. Now I really got some pressure." Prior to starting my company, I stayed celibate for about a year and a half, paid my taxes, took care of everything—I put my whole life in order. It was like preparing a racehorse to run. I give credit to Bonnie Berman, who at the time was the most visible model in the world, and she believed in me.

Probably the most important thing to me about Bethann Management was the opportunity it provided for me to become the person I am today. Did I love the agency? Did I love the kids I had? You bet I did. But really it was the opportunity to develop

my personal vision and style—to follow my own drum—that mattered. I was such a nonconformist that I didn't need to be where everybody else was. I could find comfort in a corner, far from the madding crowd. I took a chance and did something on my own—that's the stuff I have found most meaningful.

At this point in my life, I'm driven to get certain things accomplished. That's my objective. There are certain things I need to do because others will be shortchanged if I don't and because there's no one else to do these things. There's no one else to document certain things, to reveal and share certain things, or to shape certain things. There are many people in my life and lifetime who are physically gone but still with me in spirit. They are my contemporaries. There will never be another one of any of them, just as there will never be another Bethann. I owe it them and to myself to do as much as I can in the time I have left.

My documentary *Invisible Beauty* tells the simple story of an industry that most people don't know much about, about what goes on behind the scenes. I had to do the film because I wanted to finish what I'd started. I wanted to show people that there's a problem with the fashion industry because it doesn't understand how to diversify consistently by including other races. I want people to really understand that if someone believes something different, it's okay, that's cool. If someone looks different, it's okay, it's cool. To not accept diversity hurts everyone. It hurts the fashion industry. It hurts society. In my industry, I'm a person everyone can respect. I have the history. I've been around long enough. If I have to do a town hall meeting, I'll do a town hall meeting, but I'll keep on, in hopes the flame will catch and stay lit so that I don't have to worry about it anymore, so that I can lie in a hammock and rest.

The hammock is one of the most important designs that man has made. It allows a great rest after you've accomplished what you set out to accomplish for the day. I know I've got things to finish. I'm dusting and tidying up. I'm trying to tie up loose ends in my career. But that's not all of who I am. I need to see other cultures. I need to be among people who reflect more than tangible items proving financial success. That's why I live in rural Mexico. I no longer want to be stuck in a big city, with big cars, and big houses, and big things. I want to live simply, to experience the preciousness of life.

Mellody Hobson

Mellody Hobson is the president of Ariel Investments in Chicago, which she joined as an intern after graduating from Princeton University. She regularly contributes to ABC's Good Morning America *to speak on financial literacy.*

✳

I grew up in Chicago as the youngest of six children. My mother was a single mom and an entrepreneur. It's deeply imprinted on me how hard she worked. When I was a kid, I didn't go to preschool. Instead, every day until I was five, I went to work with my mom. She was in real estate and converted old buildings into condos or rental apartments. I would follow her wherever she went: If she had to take someone to court, I went to court. If she had to meet with a plumber, I just sat there while they talked. I was very content to be by myself, and I also knew how to be quiet. Very quickly, I adapted to whatever the setting dictated. It's not that I didn't talk, but growing up in that environment, I learned what was appropriate and what wasn't.

The biggest challenge for me as a child was money, something we never had a lot of. My mom would do anything to make sure that we had what we needed, but there were times when it just wasn't enough. Sometimes we got evicted; sometimes our phone got disconnected. These things left a mark, and I always tell people it's no accident that I work in the investment business, because I desperately wanted to understand money. I felt this sense of insecurity around it, which I think is why I was such an angst-ridden kid. It took me a long time just to calm down. My family's circumstances definitely taught me empathy for people who are struggling. I think many people in the financial world have this solid sense of what a capitalist is and does, yet I have this yin and yang in my brain about it, which is very much a function of feeling exposed as a kid—again, not because my mother wasn't trying but more because she was up against a lot. I believe the capitalist system works. I also believe that while it's fundamental to American society, we—as a society—are still compelled to reach back to help those our system may not have helped.

When we were kids, my mother used to tell us that if we slept past six, the world was passing us by. Now I generally wake up at four every morning. To this day, I tell my mom she's ruined sleep for me because the first thing I do when I get up in the morn-ing—I live in a high-rise—is look out the window to see how many lights are on. I always feel like there's something I should be doing, so I like to get up and get started. On an average day, by nine o'clock in the morning, I'll have gone running; done *Good Morning America*, including makeup and hair; made my way to the office; completed a radio interview; and begun work.

I was a very odd child. I was obsessive about school and never wanted to miss it. If my mother told me there was a snow day, I'd accuse her of not wanting me to get a good education. I'd make her prove it to me, show me on television that there was no school. One time my school bus got into an accident, so I got off and walked the rest of the way. I'd even ration television for myself. I'd allow myself a half-hour break from homework to watch *Happy Days*. Sometimes I'd stay up until two o'clock studying, and in the morning, my mom would say, "Don't go to school. Just rest." And I'd literally go, "Are you kidding me?" One thing my mother did absolutely right was that if it was important to me, it was important to her, no matter what it was—a science project, lunch, getting to school on time, whatever it was. And if she couldn't make it happen, she trusted I would. If I knew my mom was running late in the morning, I would take a cab by myself to school. She came to expect that I would solve the problem, and as a result, I became a very independent kid.

There are many people who inspire me personally, but if I'm intellectually hon-est with myself, it's my own head that pushes me day in and day out. Just the same, that doesn't mean there aren't influences. My business partner, John Rogers, is a huge influ-ence in my life, and I have dear, dear friends who inspire me every day—too many to even name. I say to myself, "This person is so good or so smart or so thoughtful." And

I think, "I want a little bit of this or that," and I try to figure out how to incorporate whatever it is into my life. One of our peers, another money manager, just sent back a letter that John and I wrote to him in the middle of the financial crisis—it's perfectly preserved and framed, and he signed the mat, "Nice job staying the course." In our letter, we'd told him how much we appreciated his reassurance and his confidence. Who would think to keep something like that and to send it back as a reminder? That's so thoughtful. Just so good and inspiring. I mean, how can one be that thoughtful toward others? Do you say to yourself, "I'm going to put this letter aside so that I can remind them later of this rough period?" Or do you stumble across it and think, "Wouldn't this be a nice thing to send back to them to let them see how they were thinking at the time?" I try to take something away from those experiences. I have a friend who regularly calls me and says, "What can I do to simplify your life today?" And it's a genuine offer and terribly reassuring. That's an inspiration. Could I even think of something that good and thoughtful? How can I be more like that toward another person?

In terms of my profession, I'm passionate about financial literacy. I want to live in a financially literate society. I want kids to understand the importance of savings and investing. I want to try to replicate the great savers who came out of the Depression, the best savers the country has ever seen. I try to get people to understand how much better their life is going to be when they're financially aware—it's the promise of a better life, and I can paint a really nice picture of it. I always joke that I dream wide awake. I visualize what those dreams could be. I show people what happens when you actually understand how you're spending your money and the importance of saving and investing, how these things make your life so much better and will make the lives of your children and grandchildren and nieces and nephews better—whatever that might mean. It could be as simple as not becoming a burden to them or as bold as being able to help them pay for college or buy their first house. In the words of Jesse Jackson, "Freedom is never free." There is a cost, some of which is a delay in gratification. But as most of us were taught when we were children, you can't eat dessert first.

It's crucial that people understand the importance of financial literacy, because it's actually lifesaving. It's no different from having good health. It's no different from taking care of your kids. If you don't pass down good money skills to your kids, if you yourself don't feel financially secure, it causes great anxiety. It affects your health and your ability to live comfortably. I think the worst thing you can possibly be is old and poor, because at that stage, you don't have many options. You can't go back to work. That's one of my recurring nightmares. As long as you're able-bodied, you can make money, even if it's behind the counter at McDonald's or Starbucks, or wherever. At least you have options, which you may not have when you're old. I want to make sure that those golden years are golden.

Michael Dell supposedly has a saying: "Pleased, but not satisfied." I'm pleased, but not satisfied. I know we have a special culture at Ariel Investments and a place where people from all walks of life can shine and thrive. While we work really hard to maintain that, it in no way suggests we're perfect—we've got a long, long, *long* way to go. But in the twenty years I've invested so far, in terms of my person, I've reaped more rewards than I could have ever imagined. I'm not talking about financial rewards or about being on television. I'm not talking about any of that. I'm talking about as a human being. I've been humanized by my work. It's not that I wasn't humane before, but there are so many people-related things that you deal with when you're an entrepreneur. I always joke that there's no manual. You have to think on your feet and from your heart because people's lives and livelihoods are often at stake. Managing people's money is serious business. We invest a lot of time and energy into educating our clients. Charles Schwab likens it to curing cancer, and he's right. I feel that our work actually makes people's lives better. It allows them to send their kids to college. It allows them to retire comfortably. All of that is inspiring work.

Though there aren't many women of color in my field, there are some amazing success stories, including Edith Cooper at Goldman Sachs and Carla Harris at Morgan Stanley. I think there are a lot of reasons why the number is so small. Like all things, it's hard to be different in a particular environment. I once had someone tell me that I'm both nonthreatening to others and nonthreatened, a balance that's hard to maintain. Either people become too threatening or they are too threatened, and some get shaken out because of it—not because they're not smart or talented, but because, in this business, you're always swimming upstream. And I don't say that as a victim in any way. I just know there's a challenge, I'm up to it, and I believe there are lots and lots and *lots* of black women who are up to it, too.

My ultimate heroes are Martin Luther King, Jr., Nelson Mandela, and Gandhi. They're in a class of their own, at the top of any list. They gave up so much for other people. Then there's Marian Wright Edelman, whom I've interviewed. At the end of an unbelievable talk, I asked her, "What do you regret?" She replied, "That I haven't done enough," and I literally burst into tears. It was like, "If *you* haven't done enough, then what have I done?" I mean, I'm so amazed by her. She's a warrior for others.

My mother has been a quiet hero. She's shy but has very high standards, which I appreciate about her and probably haven't told her enough. She taught me not to settle. When I was a little kid, she used to say over and over and over again, "Be the labor great or small, do it well or not at all." This ethic is part of me, and I thank her for that.

The teachers I had as a kid and today's teachers, they're genuinely, unabashedly invested in kids. They are heroes, and there are lots of them.

I look at the president and the First Lady, who are not only raising a family but also representing our country—our larger family—so well around the world. I think they're amazing people. I remember when President Obama was debating in the election, and I thought, "He was put on Earth to make me a better person." It wasn't even political; it was the remarkable way he handled himself in the face of a difficult situation. I mean, how do you stand there, under such pressure, smiling and looking so unaffected and calm and charming? I love, *love* Obama's statement that "There's never been anything false about hope." I made that my Christmas card one year.

My current state of mind is curious and open. I'm working really hard not to be so hardwired about everything, to be more consciously open to whatever comes along. I want to make sure that I'm asking enough questions, because you can't learn enough. I'm reading a book on Einstein now, which I'm relishing. Einstein believed that creativity is more important than anything else, and he thought that science itself has suffered from a lack of creativity because most scientists build on the work of others instead of blowing open an idea themselves. The other thing about Einstein that is so interesting

to me is that he was genuinely happy. If you look, he was often photographed smiling. He was a happy person, and that's something that's underrated. People don't appreciate what happiness does for those around them, let alone for themselves.

The thing about life is that it's like the song "My Way" that Frank Sinatra sang: "Regrets, I've had a few / But then again, too few to mention." I feel the same way. A lot of the things I regret having done, or would do differently if given the chance, were probably a function of age, of a lack of either knowledge or maturity. I don't know if I could have gotten where I am now any faster. Life gives you the lesson first, and sometimes it comes really, really hard. Generally, my regrets have to do with people: Could I have said something better? Could I have been nicer? Could I have been more compassionate or empathetic? I do think these things sometimes, and I know when I do, I probably could have done a better job at whatever it was. At the same time, I'm only human and don't always say or do things perfectly.

I'm happy with my work now, and hopefully what's next is evolving and growing and learning. I mean, how much capacity does the human mind have to grow? From where I am, it's exponential! Every decade I have to learn something new. Right now, I'm in the decade of swimming. Last decade was running. It's all really fun and exciting. I wonder what I'll do next. Maybe I'll learn to play the piano. Maybe I'll climb Kilimanjaro. I want to try it all.

Janice
Bryant Howroyd

Janice Bryant Howroyd is the CEO of ACT-1, the largest minority-woman-owned employment agency, which she founded in 1978. In 2005 she received the Spirit of American Enterprise Presidential Award, and in 2008 she was named Entrepreneur of the Year by BET.

✳

Many of my memories of childhood in a small Southern town are filled with the smells of cooking, gardens, and summer rains. They are lavish in family and community. Family dinners especially come to mind. We were eleven siblings, Mama and Daddy, and whoever happened to drop in. We always sat together at the table, and prayer rotated from child to child each day. Inevitably, one of my brothers would interrupt with a sharp "Amen!" because he was ready to get started. Mama would express that she was "undone with such disrespect for our Lord," and depending on how much laughter the culprit received, Daddy would make him either stand to the side of the table and wait to eat, or do the dishes. As dishes were considered a girls' chore in our family, we girls always chanted, "Dishes! Dishes! Dishes!"

Our community was tight-knit. In the fifties, sixties, and seventies, everybody knew everybody in Tarboro, North Carolina. Or at least everybody on our side of the tracks knew everybody else on our side of the tracks. The Norfolk Southern Railway system, which is a remnant of the prosperous Southern tobacco industry, runs right through the middle of the town and continues to service freight. When I was growing up, segregation was the order of the day: The east side of the tracks was an all-black neighborhood and the west side of the tracks was all white—mostly Protestant, with a few Catholics and, I think, two or three Jewish families.

As a child in a small Southern town, I was somewhat sheltered. However, I do remember reading a magazine article in which John Lennon was quoted as saying he thought the world's problems could be solved if people of different races mingled and married and created children together. His assumption, I think, was that we all love our children. That idea really affected me, as I'd never thought about race as an opportunity to blend and unite on issues before that.

We did not have a library on our side of town, and so, when I reached junior high, my parents allowed me to cross the tracks to borrow books from the white library, which by then had begun to lend to black children. I would always wait until dusk to stroll home so that on the way I could peek into the windows of the grand old Southern homes that graced Main Street. When I got home, my mom would be standing by the door, waiting to pull me into our house with admonishments and threats she never intended to keep. Walking down Main Street and glimpsing bits of white life was worth my mother's feigned irritation.

"A family that prays together stays together." That little saying embodies how we lived. Everybody began everything with prayer. In the mornings, we prayed over home-cooked breakfasts. Dinners were prayer competitions. We also had chores, divided up along gender lines. The older children were responsible for babysitting the younger ones and for helping them with their homework. Sunday, the Sabbath, meant rest, Sunday school, and evening church. Big Sunday dinners were not just a family ritual, they were a community ritual.

Reading was my big thing. At night, it was common for Daddy to pass through for lights-out checks and catch me reading, by flashlight under the covers, the books I'd borrowed from the white library. He'd harrumph, and I'd put out the light long enough for him to leave. And then as soon as he was out the door, I'd turn it back on and go to wonderful places and experience wonderful things until dawn. Books were like food to me, and I read everything I could get my hands on. My favorites as a child were my aunt Sarah's *Encyclopedia Britannica* and any autobiography or biography. Today, I still love biographies, as well as the Bible and James Allen's *As a Man Thinketh.*

We got our first television set in the late sixties. Everyone in the neighborhood stood and watched as it was delivered. Daddy allowed us to watch a bit of TV back then. We had such an established routine of study, chores, and prayer that it didn't stand a chance of competing. Besides, we'd learned to live without it. We would run through the neighborhood to tell family and friends whenever someone black was going to be on. Back then, blacks in my hometown were still called "Negroes," and we marveled at how good they looked on-screen. The first time I saw Diahann Carroll as Julia on *Julia*, I thought she looked like a porcelain doll. She's still so gorgeous!

Many of the values emphasized in our home are addressed in my book, *The Art of Work: How to Make Work, Work for You!* Education was stressed. We grew up with the saying "Education is freedom." We were a highly spiritual family and community, and we lived by old-fashioned rules. Today, many of my parents' guiding principles might be seen as sexist, but they worked for the time and place we were in, and we were always taught to challenge what we thought was not right. Mamma and Daddy believed that leadership should occur by example. I realize now, far more than I did then, that they worked together in a very special way to co-lead our family. Mamma got her degree by going to night school after Daddy got home, yet she never missed a beat as a housewife and mother. Daddy showed his affection for her in overt and constant ways. They taught us what a solid and rewarding marriage can be, as well as not to settle for less than what you want in life for yourself and from others.

Growing up in a town where grown men subsidized family incomes by cutting grass, I was aware early on of the value of work and a solid job. The career people in my hometown were the teachers and preachers. My goal was to be a social worker, and in a sense, I've become that through both my core work and my community work. Throughout my life, I've been conscious of the fact that I have opportunities that many people before me—many African Americans and many women, period—did not have. Fulfilling my goals enables me to create new opportunities to help others achieve their dreams. This desire continues to drive me, and I still love learning how far I can go by supporting those around me. The perks of success aren't just the "stuff" you can afford; the perks are the abilities you gain to influence people, politics, and opportunities for others.

When I arrived in Los Angeles after graduating from college, I couldn't get a job because I was considered "overqualified." My brother-in-law encouraged me to hang my own shingle after I reorganized his office and hired the appropriate people to staff it. Since then, I've escorted thousands of people out of bad career decisions and into new opportunities through our AppleOne offices. Through our Agile-1 Solutions, I've assisted companies across the globe in planning, implementing, maintaining, and sustaining effective workforce solutions. This means dealing with different cultures, time zones, and challenges. It means caring for people I've never met and affecting their lives in dynamic ways. It often means being weary of airports and meetings, yet it also means waking to the promise of opportunity not only for me but for someone else. That's a pretty great reward for a few extra hours of work.

From day one, my family has celebrated my dream. Many of my siblings have worked at my company in summer jobs, and several are now executives. God has been good to me. My husband and I are so happy that our children have elected to go into our business. They're doing exceptionally well and are respected by the other team members. That both of our children find it a joy and honor to work with us speaks to our comfortable relationship and to the respect they have for me as a professional and as a parent.

My mother-in-law said something very wise when my husband and I were first engaged and I asked her opinion on raising children. She told me, "Your children pay more attention to what you do than what you say." It was great advice then, and I've continued to live by it. The key ingredient to raising children, whether as a working mom or a stay-at-home mom, is respect: Respect your children enough to give them the information and guidance that they show readiness to grow from. Respect yourself enough to honor the decision you make to work in or out of the home. Respect the work you do as valuable and allow your children to see and experience you doing it. There need not be a strict line of separation between work and home life. All things have their place and time, which in today's world can be fluid. Allow your children to be as inquisitive about what you do for a living as they are about the sun, food, and every other little thing they wonder about. Provide solid answers and never make them feel guilty about the fact that you work to support them. Celebrate your work and let them know you work because of the decisions you've made along the way. Don't make yourself out to be a martyr.

My greatest achievement to date is learning to love myself the way God designed me. As my career has evolved, I've needed to address all the isms, including racism and sexism. The most challenging among them, however, has been learning to get-out-of-my-own-way-ism. It's not what they call you that matters, but who you answer to. I truly believe I can do all things through Christ, who strengthens me, and this faith has been monumental in my journey and key to my success.

I never had that one big break along the way. Rather, I've kept creating opportunities, one customer at a time. If I were offered the chance to do something professionally other than what I'm doing now, I would not change my career. However, I would change how I approached it in some way. Many people say they wouldn't do anything differently, but I'm not one of them. If I had to do it over again, I'd love myself fully, as God loves me, a lot sooner. Has anyone ever told you, "If it don't kill ya, it'll strengthen ya"? Well, the passion for and faith in something bigger than you, the commitment to serving more than just yourself, can keep you going. I mean, a mother can lift a car off her child because she's motivated to save that child's life. Being born into circumstances that have consistently required more effort, more tries, and more faith than the circumstances of many others has made me who I am. As I've never known what it means to achieve from an easy place, I expect more of myself and deliver it as a normal process.

In my industry, there are many, many women of color. Ours is not a field, however, in which I see many African American women starting and growing their own businesses. Though the advance of technology fosters a more level playing field, at some point, face-to-face negotiations take place and the old isms pop up. Thankfully, being prepared, offering a high-value product, and trusting yourself continue to break down barriers to opportunity and to success.

Today, I'm enjoying the successes and challenges of living globally. My company is expanding into more than thirty countries, and many of our clients require visits as well as structure and strategy. It's exciting, and I'm getting a kick out of leading a company that designs and delivers workforce solutions to companies across the globe. Escorting people to job and career opportunities in the United States and abroad is particularly fulfilling right now, as jobs are a top issue.

Beyond work, my passion is education. In my business, I see the results, good and bad, of the education system and the manner in which students gain — or do not gain — advantage from it. My family and I provide financial support to North Carolina Agricultural and Technical State University, and to the University of Southern California, and we donate scholarship money to other schools. As a woman, I'm proud and honored to support organizations such as the Women's Business Enterprise National Council, the National Minority Supplier Development Council, and the National Association of Women Business Owners. It's a joy to support the work of the PhD program, and needless to say, by doing business in so many communities, we're supporting organizations across the country and the globe.

Perhaps I could be described as living on passion because I'm passionate about everything I do. Everything inspires me. I have good passions, which are fundamentally positive, and what I call "yuck" passions, or the things I'm trying to change because I care about them deeply. Good passions are work, community enrichment through education, and most of all, my family. Yuck passions include what I consider to be the current divide in governments across the globe that have become ugly instead of productive.

I awake every morning to love and expectation. Meditation always puts me in a peaceful state. No matter where I am in the world, I meditate prior to sleeping and immediately upon waking. This practice is built into my life. Life makes me smile. Faith promises, and it delivers, as long as I stay grounded in the principle that "Faith, without works, is dead." Conversely, faith, with works, is alive.

Faith, family, and fortitude are necessities for me. Beyond a doubt, my family, especially my parents, have been the biggest influence in my life. As an adult, my husband, Bernie, and our children have been added to that list. My family, especially my husband, have always been right there to offer love, encouragement, a shoulder to cry on, and perspective along the way.

"I can do all things through God, Who strengthens me." Mama and Daddy gave me that verse and taught its meaning by their example. Everyone who knows me knows that my heroes are my mother and my daughter, Katharyn. My heroes are my husband and our son, Brett. My mother and my father were my strongest mentors, and my older sister, Sandy, was absolutely awesome as I approached my teen years, as well as after I'd grown up and moved to California to live near her. My role model has always been my mother. She is just so, so perfect to me. She has taught me what it means to be a complete person and be unafraid of my own power. Lately, my daughter has been a role model as well. She has accomplished so much yet remains sweet and true to her personal standards. The relationships I have with my family, friends, business, community, and myself—framed by my faith—are my most valuable treasures.

Iman

Iman began modeling during college and quickly became a supermodel and muse to many prominent designers. In 1994, after two decades of modeling, Iman launched her own cosmetics line that focuses on hard-to-find shades for ethnic women.

✳

I am the woman I am today in all respects because of Africa. I was born and raised in Mogadishu, Somalia. As I wrote in my book, *I Am Iman*, "I get my stubborn character from my country's shape. Somalia is situated in the Horn of Africa at the eastern-most projection of the continent. I relate to the world in much the same way that Somalia relates to Africa. I am African, but I also stick out a bit." I was the first girl born in three generations in my family, and my arrival was a very big occasion. My grandfather traveled from Ethiopia to Somalia to celebrate my arrival. First my parents named me Zahra, but my grandfather decided to change my name to Iman. He said I should have a masculine name. Iman means "to have faith in God." My family had a great deal of faith, and I have always had faith. I have become my name. And I am my father's daughter. I have four siblings, and I am the only one who looks identical to my father. I am very close to my father, and he instilled in me the belief that there was nothing I could not do as a girl. I was not raised to go off with the richest man. I was taught that I could do what the boys in my family could do, that the sky— and beyond—was the limit. Even though Somalia is filled with strong, progressive, and educated girls, the society's ultimate intention is to marry girls off. And Somalia being a Muslim country, the father decides when a girl will marry. But that was out of the question for my father—he and my mother always believed it was my choice whom to marry.

My parents sent me to an all-girls boarding school because it offered the best education. As a young girl, I did not understand that my mother and father were trying to make sure I got as much of an education as possible. All I knew was I was the only one in my family being sent away. I ended up being a straight-A student, and my father loved the fact that I was a better student than my brothers. He used to ask them, "Why can't you be more like Iman?" My father always fought against sexism. He believed the fight started at home, with girls being treated well before going out into society, so that if society tries to stifle them they will be prepared to flourish nonetheless.

At the time of the 1969 Somali coup, my family was living in Saudi Arabia, as my father was the ambassador there. Quickly all the embassies were closed; my parents returned to Somalia, and my brothers and I were pulled from school. For many months, our family was living in uncertainty about our future, as members of the old government started to disappear. Around us, my father's friends were executed, arrested without being charged with any crimes, and put under house arrest. We were terrified; we waited for my father to be taken away as well. While we were in limbo, unsure of our fate, my mother was secretly planning our family's escape. One evening she called all of us together and said, "It's time for us to get out of here because your father might be the next to disappear." She then informed us that we would be leaving our home later that night, that we were not allowed to bring anything with us, and that we would not be returning. I was not scared. Rather, I felt a resigned acceptance. As the children of diplomats, we had moved so much that there was a part of me that was simply used to it. When it was pitch-black that night, an old VW van with no seats in the back arrived at our home. The driver instructed us to lie down and cover ourselves with blankets and not to sit up under any circumstances. We drove through the night, and by sunrise we had arrived in Kenya. We actually crossed over the border by foot. Suddenly we were refugees asking for asylum, and the Kenyan government granted it to us. We were free, yet we had no food, no home, and we had left all our possessions in Somalia. We were destitute. The money and valuables my family previously had were used on bribes to get us to freedom.

My father was heartbroken. Everything he had worked his entire life to achieve as a respected diplomat and government official had been taken away from him—his home, his status, his land—and he had nothing to give his children. I was only fifteen, and a part of me viewed our new circumstances as an adventure, but I idolized my father and he was in pain, and there was nothing I could do to make him better.

When I was around sixteen years old, I asked to go to Nairobi University. I was allowed to, but I had to pay for my own tuition. I ended up becoming a translator of brochures for Italian and French tourists visiting Nairobi, and a waitress, in order to pay for school. During my first year in Nairobi, this man, who turned out to be the world-renowned photographer Peter Beard, stopped me in the street and asked me, "Have you ever been photographed?" I thought he was trying to pick me up, so I kept on walking and didn't pay any attention. I was just a political science student on my way to campus. Even though I didn't answer him at first, he kept asking me and started walking with me. To get rid of him I said, "Yes, of course I have." And in my mind I was thinking, "What do these people think, I have never seen a camera?!" After much back and forth, I agreed to let him take my picture in exchange for the cost of my tuition, which I think was around the equivalent of eight thousand dollars. He accepted, and that was my first negotiation. And at that point in 1975, I had never seen a fashion magazine in my life. I had never worn makeup before. I had never worn heels.

Most importantly, I had never heard of modeling. But I ended up taking these pictures with Peter at a ranch outside of Nairobi. I didn't want to go off alone with this man, so I brought a friend along for the shoot. My parents knew nothing of what I was doing. They would have completely disapproved. They had plans for me, and modeling was not one of them. I remember feeling very uncomfortable and very unnatural. But I just followed Peter's instructions. After he took my photographs, I thought that was the end of that, and I went on with my life. I went back to school completely unaware that back in New York the star-making machine was in motion.

When Peter left Kenya, I had no idea what he was going to do with the photographs, and I did not care as long as my parents never found out. They would have never approved of the images, in which I was nude from the waist up, with traditional necklaces and my hands covering my breasts. In the world of modeling they are considered "artful nudes," but my father would have called them something else. Peter showed the photographs to Wilhelmina Cooper, one of the top modeling agents in America. When I talked to her after Peter called me, she told me she would love for me to join her agency. I asked her, "What does that require?" and she said, "You have to move to New York. We will send you a plane ticket." I said to myself, "I can go there, check it out, and come back." Never did I consider going there and staying. I was not yet eighteen. I needed permission from my parents to leave the country. I didn't have a passport. But there was nothing that was keeping me in Nairobi.

So I forged the date on my birth certificate, paid for a passport, and got tickets for myself and for a friend to come with me. My parents didn't know; they were a country away, in Tanzania. I thought I would just go to New York for a couple of days. But when I arrived at the Wilhelmina agency, Peter had other plans for me. The next day there was a press conference with over sixty members of the media. Apparently three months before I arrived, some journalist had written a full-page article about this model coming to New York that Peter had discovered. The article was accompanied by a full-page picture of me—a full page! I still have it somewhere in my office. What Peter said in the article was, "She doesn't speak a word of English." Of course, he made this up. Yet still, I went along with the charade. I played my part just like Peter played his. Looking back, I often wonder if I really had a choice. When I arrived in America, I was in the country illegally and I did not know a single person besides Peter. I felt like I had no choice, no way to back out of the deal I had already made. Before the press conference, he told me about this sham and I said, "How are we going to do this? They are going to find out that I not only speak English but I speak several other languages." But Peter's story was much better for publicity. Once the press conference began, Peter fumbled around for a while pretending to translate for me, but I didn't speak Swahili and Peter didn't speak Somali. After this went on for a bit, one of the reporters asked Peter a question, and I decided to respond, "Why don't you ask me yourself?" And the reporter focused on me at that point and asked, "So, you speak English?" and I answered, "Yes." Then he asked me, "Why didn't you say so?" And I told the crowd, "Because it makes a better story." And the press ran with that story.

As soon as I arrived in New York, I was the It Girl. Literally my third day in New York, before I even got my full work visa, I had my first gig. I went right to the top. The seed of Iman Cosmetics was even planted on that third day in New York. I was at my first booking, where I had no idea what was going on, and the makeup artist came up and asked me the most perplexing question. There were two of us models, and he asked only me, "Did you bring your own foundation?" I didn't know what he was talking about because I had never worn it, and even when I was doing the pictures with Peter, I had no makeup on. I really had no idea what he was talking about. So he proceeded to mix something up and put it on my face. When I looked at myself in the mirror, I looked gray. I couldn't understand why I looked so different. The pictures, thankfully, were in black and white. By the time they were published, I knew a little bit more of what was happening, and I tried to keep a grasp of things so they didn't spiral out of my control. Things were getting a little out of hand because I didn't know much besides what Wilhelmina and Peter told me about the industry. Even then I knew it was important that I be in control of my own destiny.

Something that was instilled in me growing up in my family was the importance of always knowing my worth. And people in the business could see that about me. Many young models when they are starting out will say yes to everything. And people felt that I was in a position to walk away from it all. I didn't feel that people in the industry were doing me a favor, nor did I feel like I was doing them a favor. I felt like we were starting from the same position. I never felt like I was less, and I have always made them feel that way about me. I don't have to compromise. And I think that's what propelled me and gave me longevity in my career as a model. I have always known my self-worth. I have never compromised, and that came from my parents.

Far too often as women, we are not told that we have self-worth, and that is doubly so as a model—you have nothing. The editor decides, the photographer, hair and makeup—everyone decides how you look. Everyone decides except you. But the basis of my whole life has been to know my self-worth, which is a belief I try to instill in others, especially young girls. My ten-year-old daughter, like so many young girls, is scared to say no for fear that somebody won't like her. I tell my daughter,

"It's okay if they don't like you. If they don't like you, they are not worth being in your life."

With my first year of modeling income, I was able to buy my parents a home and pay off my brother's tuition. Modeling just became a job. It wasn't like, "Oh, I love this work." To me it was just a job that would allow me to do things I would never be able to do working as a waitress. And for a while, that's how I felt, but by my third year, when I went to do the European collection, modeling became a career for me. Before that, I was primarily a magazine model, and then I started to do runway. And it became fun and I started to become close to the designers and came to understand the business more, and I started to care more about modeling. So I stayed because of the people in the business, the friendships I made with people like Bethann Hardison, which made it worthwhile.

Runway was much more fun for me than doing print. I could become any character and actually *be*, rather than have it be about what the photographer could capture. Photographers can capture a moment even when you are still, but with runway, there is the audience, and they make the decision what you are. It's the difference between film and theater. One is about the editing and the lighting, and the other is about that live performance. That's what runway is: live theater. Or live fashion, so to speak.

During my modeling days, there was this need within the industry to control the images that would be turned out by the models, and black beauty was treated as if there could only be one black model at a time. At that time in the seventies, there were two or three black photography models, not runway models, working at the same time. When I came on the scene, the top model was Beverly Johnson. People acted like I had to dethrone Beverly and take her spot, as if we couldn't be in the industry at the same time. But there were lots of Caucasian models working at the same time. Beverly and I actually became friends, but at the time they treated her like, "Good-bye, Beverly. Someone is going to take your place." The industry kept this tension going between black models. I was the first one not to play that game.

The way I rebelled against the norms of the industry was by making myself a very important part of the decision-making process. During that time, when they did ads, there was a quota to be made. If there were three models, one of them had to be black, but they didn't care about equality. It was just a quota that had to be met. But I would not be their quota. They could not get that out of me. I made myself worthy. What I was always scared of is for black models to become an exchangeable commodity and become disposable, so I was a professional, no matter what. Leverage is nothing if you don't deliver. Because at the end of the day, image is my currency. As a fashion model, I have to bring the client arresting, irresistible images. When they think about the hair and the makeup and everything, we're like backgrounds, we're like extras. And I wanted to be the leading lady. So to prove to them that I was the leading lady, I had to steal the light from them—not from the black girls, but from the white girls who are already the leading ladies. I was competing with the white models, and they didn't understand how I crept up on them. And black models really didn't like me from the beginning because I said I didn't really view myself as a black model or a black woman. And this is the reason: I came from a country where no one ever called me a black woman. Before I came to the United States, I had never been called a black woman; I was just a woman. So the clients didn't think I was stealing the white girls' modeling jobs, but it started shifting, and soon I started taking jobs from white girls!

The advice I give young black models is always to have a plan A and a plan B. The number of models and the number of young girls who want to become models is astronomical compared with the ones who actually make it in the business. I always tell them they should know that from the start. Just because you are the most beautiful girl in town doesn't necessarily mean you should be a model. It's a different thing; sometimes modeling has nothing to do with beauty. So you have to understand that. I also tell the young black models to come in with their own personal style. They should never think they are going to be the next Gisele or Tyra. We already have them. We need the next somebody else. We need the next you. We need the best of you—bring that to the front and don't be scared of it. Be comfortable in your own skin. Modeling is a blank canvas, with photographers, editors, makeup artists, and you projecting a story. It is part of our job to change, to be ever evolving. We don't look the same on every page and in every month. Embrace that change, invite that change, and don't run from it. And if it's not working out, give yourself a time limit of three to five years, and if you are not hitting what you think you should be hitting, then move on. That is the thing people don't understand. They think it's right around the corner. It's not about how much talent they have, because a girl can come in who has never done anything in her life and can become a star overnight because she has the right look at the right moment. So always have a plan A and a plan B. If you're young, finish school. This is a career that eats its young, and it will spit them back out, and they need to be prepared for something else when that happens.

My transition out of modeling came in the form of Iman Cosmetics. I never forgot my first shoot, when the makeup artist put foundation on that made me look gray. Through the years, I mixed and matched blends for myself so the same thing wouldn't happen again. I went to Woolworth's and bought every foundation I could see that had a little bit of any tint, whether it was golden or red or whatever, as long as it wasn't beige, and then I started mixing and making foundation. I would put it on my face and take a Polaroid to see how it photographed on my skin. So I would take pictures of me in different variations of foundations and I would keep that mix with me in my bag. I never went to a shoot without foundation again; I never wanted a white makeup artist to make me look gray again. Luckily, as I became more successful I was able to introduce black makeup artists and hairdressers into our midst.

When Iman Cosmetics officially launched in 1994, it was instantly a success with magazine editors and celebrities, but most importantly it was a success with regular women. I could see that everybody was talking about multicultural this, global that, and in the streets of Manhattan there was a whole new generation of kids who dressed differently and acted differently, who didn't see whether they were black or white or anything in between. I couldn't tell who was what, but it was a new generation, and I thought that would be the way to go with my line. And so that's what I wanted to base the cosmetics on, the new multiculturalism. Iman Cosmetics introduced makeup for a new generation of women with skin of color—a uniquely diverse group that included all ethnicities, mixed races, and virtually every complexion under the sun. It was true globalism. No contouring, no spackling, no changing your face. The joy of makeup is enhancing your natural beauty—making choices. Find the need; fulfill the need! I had the emotional and psychological attachment to it, to us, to women with skin color. I knew there was a huge gap in the marketplace: millions of other women like me, and not just black women, but Asian, Latina, and multiethnic women—women who want makeup that celebrates us! Iman Cosmetics truly is for more than just black women. Everyone would say, "How are Asians of color?" And I would say to them, "Have you been to the Philippines? They are as black as I am!" When I was writing my book, *The Beauty of Color*, I was trying to highlight celebrities from Jennifer Lopez to Halle Berry to Cameron Diaz—a new generation of people who don't fall into the category of black or white in determining beauty, but are simply beautiful. The philosophy I built Iman Cosmetics on was that it was for "Skin of Color." In starting any business, you need to know the market research and you need to know exactly what you are talking about and you have to be able to back it up. At the end of the day it's about the product, the product, the product, and people will only buy it at the beginning because my name is on it. But if they take it home and they don't like it, then that is the end of that.

I think people responded to Iman Cosmetics because it's not about ethnicity, it's about skin tone, and we come in myriad colors. In my family alone, my two other sisters and I are all different shades. I am very political about it because the whole thing to me is about beauty, you know: What makes a blonde-haired, blue-eyed woman the beauty of the day, and of the decade? I call it "the Politics of Beauty," the cultural-cum-political power of good looks. We must give young girls a jump start on appreciating what their beauty is. It's beauty on your own terms, celebrating your own features. I would never explain how to make an African American girl's nose look smaller or slimmer or how to make an Asian's eyes look wider. Own it! Redefine it!

Through the years people have come up to me and told me I should start a clothing line, but I always thought my legacy was Iman Cosmetics. So, going beyond my second act, I didn't want anything to damage the legacy of Iman Cosmetics. It wasn't until Mindy Grossman at HSN called me and asked me to create a brand for HSN that I gave another line a lot of thought. I looked at my closet and how I dressed, and I realized I was actually more attached to my shoes and handbags than my clothes. Sometimes I pick up a bag and I will work my clothing around that bag. I am an accessories girl at heart. So that's what I built IMAN Global Chic around. I named the brand Global Chic because I didn't want the brand to be perceived as only black. My goal was to set up the building blocks, the DNA, of the brand before I went back into the big area of cosmetics and skin care.

I am proud that as a model I was most known as someone who has a great deal of integrity. I am proud of my children and my long-lasting marriage, and most of all, I am proud of myself. I grew up to be the woman I wanted to be: somebody who is caring, helpful, kind; someone who is reliable and has not lost her sense of humor.

Judith Jamison

Judith Jamison was the artistic director of Alvin Ailey American Dance Theater from 1989 to 2011. The onetime muse of Ailey himself, Ms. Jamison took over the company upon his death. Under her direction the company reached new heights, moving into a permanent space and celebrating its fiftieth anniversary with a global tour.

★

I was born in 1943, so I'm a war baby—I'm not a baby boomer. The 1940s and 1950s were a difficult time to grow up. My brother and I were among the first black kids to be integrated into our elementary school. From an early age, we had to be grounded in who we were. My parents made sure that we understood as much of our history as they could give to us, even though at that time, some black families were hesitant to discuss the past because it was so painful. I didn't get a chance to ask my grandmother or grandfather the things that I wanted to until much later in their lives. Often, these things weren't talked about because we were only a hop, skip, and a jump beyond slavery.

I grew up in a marvelous row house in Germantown, a neighborhood in Philadelphia. My maternal grandparents lived next door. My aunt lived five blocks away. My cousins and another aunt and uncle lived in West Philadelphia. We were all pretty tight. We were near and dear to each other, and caring for one another was emphasized. Family was very important, and we had wonderful family celebrations—Thanksgivings, Christmases, and Easters. Everybody would come together. Granddaddy would always say a long prayer, and even though we were hungry, we'd wait for him to finish (as if we had a choice!). Family, taking care of each other, education, and just plain old knowledge of self and understanding—those were the most important things.

Some of my strongest memories from childhood are of Mother Bethel AME Church, which is a historic church in Philadelphia. You had to be there every Sunday, and there were no excuses. That was the command, the demand, and the mantra of the Jamison family, as was traditional among African American families back then. I also remember going to the Philadelphia Museum of Art, which is one of my favorite places in the world. I love that museum. I imagined all museums looked like that until I got on a plane and went someplace else. And dance, of course, was absolutely key to my childhood. Marion Cuyjet was my teacher. She opened the door to so many little black children wanting to study ballet. In the forties, fifties, and sixties, there just weren't any places for black children to study classical ballet, yet she taught it, along with jazz, tap, and the technique of Katherine Dunham, which is a blend of African and Caribbean movements. I was exposed to a lot growing up.

When I was six, I got onstage for the first time. I was dressed in a red-checked shirt, dungarees, and pink ballet shoes. The song was "I'm an Old Cowhand from the Rio Grande," and my sister students and I did a couple of ballet steps. We all got out there — about six or seven of us. I remember being on the stage and being scared as the lights went on and the music started. I couldn't see anything. I did the steps, and then the lights went out, the curtains came down, and I heard that applause. I heard the applause, thank you, and that was it. I loved it. It was a subconscious thing. It wasn't like, "Oh, wow! I love this, Mom." I didn't say that, but in retrospect, it's what I felt. People applauded! I got over the debilitating fear and learned to trust the good fear that comes before doing something big. As long as you're creating something, there's always going to be a certain amount of "I've not been in this territory before" fear, but that's when courage comes in. I learned that lesson right quick.

The teachers who influenced me were major — and I mean major — in my concept of being out in the world. My parents gave me the foundation; my church gave me the shield, the armor, and the how-to to carry myself through life. My teachers were my mentors. I left Philadelphia for Fisk University in Nashville, Tennessee, where I spent a year and a half before returning to attend the University of the Arts, called the Philadelphia Dance Academy back then. As a student, I realized that I wanted to dance more than I wanted to teach — traditionally, the school produced more teachers than performers — and that I wasn't getting in enough performance time. In 1963 I saw Alvin Ailey dance for the first time. He and the Alvin Ailey American Dance Theater performed at the Walnut Street Theatre, and my entire class went to see them. Our improvisation class the next day was certainly tempered by what we saw in *Revelations*.

I never aspired to dance the rest of my life. That thought never crossed my mind. I knew that I wanted to have as much fun as possible, to enjoy myself, and to leave my mark on the map. I knew that I wanted to say, "We were here, and we want you to know that we were here." That desire certainly influenced my decision to accept Alvin Ailey's invitation to join the company. I knew that each performance brought me closer and closer to public acclaim, to affirmation of Alvin's genius, and to acknowledgment as a dancer among his fabulous dancers. That's always been the case. I didn't aspire to a career; I aspired to be the best dancer I could be. I was proud to celebrate the African American culture and modern dance tradition of our country. I aspired to have that written about and historically remembered, a vibrant entity in the past, present, and future — all of which I still aspire to. When you're in it, you can't see the forest for the trees. You're just in it. You're a participant and constantly trying to be extraordinary at what you're doing. That takes exquisite training. It takes commitment and dedication.

I got to New York because of Agnes de Mille. I was at the University of the Arts taking a million, billion classes. It was eight o'clock at night, and I didn't want to take this last class of the day because I was exhausted. Reluctantly, I went with a friend. At the end of the class, Ms. de Mille asked me to come to New York and be a guest dancer with American Ballet Theatre. The ballet *The Four Marys*, which includes black performers, was being revived. There were four Marys, and one of them was me. The lead was Carmen de Lavallade, who became my dear mentor. It's an old Southern plantation story, in which the "massa" falls in love with the slave, and a love story, as much as you could have that kind of love story in the time of slavery. It was a nice ballet. There are pictures of me standing on the stage in dress rehearsal, in my first fitted costume from a major house, looking like I'm two years old. ABT was among the premier ballet companies, and it was my first job.

Once the ballet was over, however, the bubble burst because there just weren't many parts for black people at ABT. *The Four Marys* was a special case, and once ABT was finished doing it, I was out the door. Fortunately, there was a woman named Martha Johnson, who was married to an extraordinary man named Stretch Johnson, who was a tap dancer and a political activist. Martha told me about an audition for the great Donald McKayle, who was doing a Roaring Twenties TV special starring Harry Belafonte and Paula Kelly, an actress who would go on to be in *Sweet Charity* and *The Andromeda Strain*. I took the audition and was terrible. But as I headed out to call my mother from across the street, I passed a man who had seen me audition. Three days later, he called me. The man was Alvin Ailey, and that's how I came to join the Alvin Ailey American Dance Theater.

I was invited into the company in 1965, and Alvin created some powerful solos and ballets for me and the company over the years, including *Cry* in 1971. I had many solos within other ballets, but *Cry* stood out from the rest. Alvin and I never had much conversation when he was creating it for me because it was about the overall movement, not the specific steps. The meaning was known to him, though maybe not in the moment to me, but it wasn't something that he would stop to explain. There wasn't time for that, and besides, he knew it would come to me. I had no explanation, no idea that *Cry* was a birthday present for his mother, that it was "dedicated to all black women — especially our mothers." Though an explanation was published in the program, we were trying to get the dance on, and I never read program notes like that before I performed anyway. I had to keep my thoughts inside myself so I could focus on what I had to do. I mean, the man had to choreograph the whole ballet in eight days, so he just started moving. He did the steps, I repeated the steps, he did the steps, and then I followed, doing the steps again. The last two days, a cloth was brought in, which Alvin wished to represent a gelé, a baby, a stole, a floor scrub, a body, and the weight of the world.

Alvin drew inspiration from many places, including his travels. There was a step in *Cry* that we'd seen when we were in the Congo in 1967, when we did ten countries in two and a half months. He and I had gone out to a club while the war was going on.

There were mercenaries being brought through downtown Kinshasa, which is where we were performing from across the river in Brazzaville. I mean it was just crazy, but we got a step out of it. We saw young women at a club doing this movement, and they were from "the bush." We were like, "Whoa, that's fabulous," and the next thing I knew, Alvin had incorporated it into *Cry*. It's one of the most powerful moments in the entire piece.

When I went onstage in the afternoon for the *Cry* dress tech, which was about two hours before the curtain was supposed to go up, I was in an unflattering costume—an ill-fitting dress that I'd never worn before. I heard Alvin groan from the darkness of the house, and I groaned myself, so instead they sewed me into my skirt from the "Wading in the Water" part of *Revelations*. It was four years old. It was like paper. It was really falling apart, and the zipper wouldn't stay up. Someone ran out to Capezio and bought two long-sleeved leotards—they needed the extra leotard because my arms are so long the sleeves had to be extended. They cut out the back, lowered the front, and then sewed me into the skirt. And that was the *Cry* costume.

Cry is fifteen or sixteen minutes long. I'd never done it from beginning to end before the premiere, and the first time I did, I got halfway through and hit "a wall"—it was like trying to run a marathon when you've never run one before; you may be a good runner, but you've never run a marathon. That's what happened to me, and that's why there's a God, someone to hold you up that isn't *you*. As I was making the last crossover of this dance, I couldn't feel anything. I couldn't feel my legs at all. They were just moving, but somehow I got through it. The great Dudley Williams came backstage from the front of the house. He was afraid I was going to fall or just collapse. He stood in the downstage right wing, pumping the air . . . pumping the air . . . pumping the air . . . giving me all this energy. When the curtain went down, I heard a huge ovation. The curtain went up, and I heard a bigger ovation. I took my bows, but it just kept going on and on and on. Mr. Ailey came backstage and was talking to me, and the audience was still applauding. We kept thinking it was finished, but it wasn't. That ovation went on for a while. At one point Alvin said to me, "Now what?" As if to say, "What do I do for you next?" He was dead serious, too. That's how *Cry* happened, and that's how I became a "box-office modern dance star."

I'm proudest of our building—the Joan Weill Center for Dance, which is the permanent home of the Alvin Ailey American Dance Theater. There's something about that word *permanent* that really makes me feel good. We were gypsies for a long time, moving from rental space to rental space. I mean we moved from Fifty-ninth Street to Forty-fifth Street to Sixty-first Street, and then finally to our permanent home at Fifty-fifth Street and Ninth Avenue and the largest dance building in New York City—the dance capital of the world. I'm really proud of that. I'm proud because it took all of us to get there. I just happened to be at the helm at the time, but it took all of us working together to get there. Alvin actually danced in the space on which the building was erected, so his spirit is there, too. There's just so much love in that building.

I think people respond to the Alvin Ailey American Dance Theater because Alvin believed that his finest works were from his gut, that they're about being human. The company is his genius, along with his idea of repertory. His legacy is the celebration of African American cultural expression and experience—and of the way we move as Americans in the modern dance tradition. We're not just up there onstage being fancy dancers with no connection to the audience. The reason we're up there is to connect. That's the whole idea. There's a spiritual bond that happens in live performance, a bond that cannot be denied. As a dancer, you don't detach from your audience, but rather you come closer to them by identifying with them and with your mutual humanity. You just happen to have the gift of dance.

Without question, my finest work comes from deep within me, from my gut, from my heart, from my spirit, and from my soul. It comes from being quiet. On the outside, I may be going fifty thousand miles per hour, but my finest work comes from the kind of spiritual presence that Alvin Ailey and I had when he was creating *Cry*. Those were our best moments, when we spoke to each other through spirit, through intelligence, and through love.

Gayle King

Gayle King is the editor at large of O *magazine and the longtime best friend of Oprah Winfrey. She got her start as a reporter in Kansas City, Missouri, and then worked as a news anchor in Hartford, Connecticut, for eighteen years. The mother of two children, Ms. King hosted* The Gayle King Show *on OWN, and now hosts the morning show on CBS.*

★

I had a really great childhood, and as I've gotten older, it has gotten even better in my mind. My dad was an electronics engineer and worked for the government, my mother was a stay-at-home mom, and I was the oldest of four girls. We lived overseas in Ankara, Turkey, from the time I was in first grade until I was in sixth. For us, going on vacation meant going to Paris, or Rome, or Greece. I have vivid memories of being somewhere and saying to my dad, "It's *so* hot out here. All we're doing is looking at rocks. Can't we go back to the hotel and swim?" And he would say, "One day you're going to appreciate this." Of course, he was right. Now I pull out the pictures and say, "This is me in Greece in the fourth grade."

Education was emphasized in our household. If we weren't given homework at school, my dad would give it to us at home. If I told him, "I didn't get any homework today," he would say, "Oh, no? What's six times six?" I remember getting it wrong and having to stay up redoing the multiplication table over and over and over again. He would say, "See? You do have homework." Going to college was never a question. Rather, it was, what college do you want to go to?

My parents also emphasized doing the right thing. To this day, I have a solid sense of right and wrong. I know that there are gray areas, but I tend to have a strong moral compass. Somebody called my TV show the other day and said, "God, Gayle, you're such a prude." I asked, "Why am I a prude?" The caller replied, "These are just different times." I'm concerned about society's loss of core values. I really am. If we're not careful, the country will go in a really scary direction. I'm not Pollyannaish — I like to have a good time, but I think there's a way to do that, and be mischievous, without compromising your core values. How can it be that people no longer think infidelity is a big deal? That people no longer think drugs are a big deal? That people think children can talk to their parents or talk to their teachers any way they want? It's shocking to me. I was raised in a house where you treated each other, and especially adults, with respect. I don't believe that you have to follow people blindly, but we've lost a basic sense of respect for one another.

That a lawmaker can holler to the president, "You lie!" in the middle of his State of the Union address is shocking to me. Of course, President Barack Obama handled the affront graciously, but the fact that the lawmaker did what he did and thought it was okay is appalling. Whether you agree or disagree with President Obama's policies, he's entitled to basic respect. You can disagree with people's policies and issues without being rude. The first time I went to the White House, George W. Bush was in office. Though I hadn't voted for him, when I pulled up to the White House, I felt a sense of awe and reverence for his office and what his position represented to us as a people. I was honored to be there for O magazine and to be doing a story on Laura Bush.

I don't have a hard-luck story. As a child, one of the few times I felt a sense of otherness was in third grade, when my class was reading about Abraham Lincoln. This little white boy said to me, "If it wasn't for Abraham Lincoln, you'd be my slave." I remember thinking, "No, I wouldn't." There were only three black kids in the class, but it was the first time I'd ever thought of myself as different. I certainly knew I was black. There was no question about that, but I was always popular, well liked, engaged, and involved. I didn't see color in that way. Even when confronted about it, I didn't feel excluded. I just thought, "Well, that's stupid." It's not something I considered an issue. My parents never really talked to me about race. I came to realize later in life that race is something that you have to be taught.

When my children, Kirby and Will, were in elementary school, I told them about Martin Luther King, Jr., and explained that he was a man who wanted blacks and whites to live together in peace. I gave them the CliffsNotes version because Will said to me, "We're staying home for King Arthur's birthday?" I thought that was so funny and explained, "No. His name is Martin Luther King." I continued, "You know, black people and white people . . ." When they looked very confused, I said, "You know, blacks and whites. What color do you think I am?" They told me I was white and their dad was black, that one sister was white and the other was black. I thought, "Oh my God, they don't know." I was stunned. They were just guessing, and I realized that we really did have to have a conversation about race. I said, "You know, if you notice when you look at people and they have darker skin . . ." And that's when it occurred to me for the first time that you have to teach people to hate.

Later, I made sure to have the talk with my son about being a black boy, because we lived in Greenwich, Connecticut, an affluent, predominantly white suburb. I had the conversation with Will when he was about twelve, a conversation I know most white parents don't have to have with their kids: "If you ever get stopped by the police, this is what you do — you say nothing. You cooperate. By 'say nothing,' I mean don't challenge, don't mouth off. Just do what you're told, and believe me, if it's something that's unjust, we'll handle it later. Because when they look at you, they instantly see 'suspect.' They don't know you went to a good school or that you were born in this house. They don't know anything about you and their defenses go up."

I attended the University of Maryland to be close to my family, who had moved to Maryland from California during my senior year in high school. While in college, by happenstance, I got my first job in a newsroom. I've always been an extrovert, and as a student I worked in a camera store as a cashier, taking people's orders. A lot of people would come in from Channel 9, a local news station. One guy in particular was a big muckety-muck, but I didn't know it. He said, "You have a really nice voice and such a pleasant personality. Have you ever thought about being on TV?" I told him no. Then he said, "Well, we have a job open in the newsroom, for a production assistant. It's an entry-level position." I asked, "Would I have to work weekends?" He cracked up and continued, "No. As it turns out, Gayle, you wouldn't have to work weekends." So I said, "Okay. I could do that." I got the job and was hooked. It was a great opportunity. If there was a story about the president—at the time it was Jimmy Carter—I pulled the slides so the viewers could see him. I typed up the scripts. I would feed the prompter and roll it for the news. I got to see all the breaking stories, something I still get excited about. Eventually, I was able to parlay my job as a production assistant into a job as a news writer in Baltimore, which I felt was a step up because it meant I would be writing the news that the anchors would be reading.

The first time I applied to get a job as a reporter trainee, I was rejected. I remember being stunned because I knew the people who had interviewed me and they had seen what I could do. Though I trusted they liked me, I still didn't get the job. I remember going in to the news director and saying, "I just don't understand. I know that I could do this job. I look at the people chosen, and I don't understand." After letting me vent, he looked at me and said very respectfully, "You know what? Life ain't fair." That moment was life changing. All I could say was "Oh, okay. Thank you for your time." It would have been different if he'd said, "Well, so-and-so can already do such and such, and you need to work on such and such."

In that moment, I understood that things were going to happen in life that defied logic and explanation, that I had to put on my big-girl pants and suck it up, and that I'd just have to work harder the next time. The following year, I did get the position, but in the meantime, I had put together a résumé tape, which I sent around to different stations. I was very strategic about my job search. Early on, I learned that the people assisting the people in power have a lot of power, and whether you befriend them or piss them off can mean the difference between getting an interview or not. I sat there with the TV broadcast yearbook and determined there were 212 markets in the country. I could see myself in one of the top twenty to thirty, so I focused my search on them.

I ended up with three job offers and chose to work in Kansas City, Missouri, first as a reporter and then as a weekend anchor. I always say to people, "Get your foot in the door." To this day, I never pooh-pooh an internship as a step for someone, because

the right kind of person can turn something small into something huge. I can always tell who's going to make it. If you have an intern who's like, "Five o'clock, gotta go," you know that person is not going far. But cream always rises to the top. All companies and all bosses appreciate someone who's working hard and trying, someone who's willing to go above and beyond the call of duty. I don't care if you're the best plumber or the best pretzel maker. There's a guy who makes pretzels at the mall in Stamford, Connecticut, who's always so damn happy. One day I asked him, "Why are you always so happy?" He replied, "Because I love making pretzels. And I love that people smile when I give them a pretzel." His attitude just stood out. People notice people who do a good job. If you get your foot in the door, you will quickly find people willing to help you. I'm always mindful of the fact that even people in the top positions got to where they arc because somebody helped them along the way.

I still love the news. That's why it's so great to be back on television. I had worked in the news and had anchored at the CBS station in Connecticut for more than eighteen years. I was just about to re-sign my contract when the *O* magazine opportunity came up. During that time, I'd also had *The Gayle King Show,* a national program that was canceled after one season. I hadn't given up my TV anchoring job because I knew TV is fickle and there are no guarantees. I said, "I'm not giving up my news job. I'm going to do both until I figure out whether or not my show is going to work." When it didn't, I still had the news, which I've always loved doing. Soon after, Oprah called to tell me that Hearst had asked her to do a magazine. They said to her, "We need somebody in New York who really understands you and gets your vision and your voice." Oprah said to me, "Who do you think?" When I offered to think about people who might be good, Oprah continued, "It's really weird because they suggested you." I said, "I'm not giving up TV for magazines. I don't know nothing about no magazine. I'm not doing that." And she said, "Yeah, that's what I told them." We sat on the phone: "What about so-and-so?" "Nah." "How about so-and-so?" "Nah."

The next morning, as I was about to re-sign with my TV station in Connecticut, I reconsidered. I thought, "I should think about this for a second." It occurred to me that it might be kind of nice to learn something new. I knew it would mean giving up

TV, but I decided to check out Hearst anyway. I figured, "I really know how Oprah thinks, I know what she likes, and I know what works for her and what doesn't." I felt that I could be instrumental in the development of the magazine because I had what no one else had at the time—I was close to Oprah and got her vision. So I went back to Hearst and said, "You know what? I'm going to do it. I'm going to leave TV and do the magazine." I'd be starting from scratch. I didn't know the lingo. I knew nothing, but Oprah said, "Yeah, but you know me and you know a good story," which was true. So it was off to the races. At first, back then, I thought the magazine was really ours to lose because Oprah had such goodwill that people respected and admired her, but that said, we told ourselves that if we didn't deliver, they wouldn't be coming back.

Five years into the magazine, I got an opportunity to be on radio, which I had never done before. I thought, "God is giving me a way to get back into the news." I loved doing radio. So then when OWN started, people said, "God, your radio show is so good. Maybe there's a way we can put the radio on TV." Now I have *The Gayle King Show*, a radio-TV hybrid, which is great. It's live, nine to eleven every morning. My goal for the show is that I want people to feel engaged. I want them to have fun. What makes the show successful is that I take callers and allow people to participate, so they don't have that "Boy, that was a waste of my time" feeling.

When you cover a story well, even if it's not something you're interested in, you think, "Okay, I get it." For instance, I interviewed Bret Michaels, and I said to him, "You know, I'm not a rocker girl," but I started watching him before the interview, and I liked him. He'd had that aneurysm and then the heart problem, and then I saw his little girls and I told him, "I just like you and I really wanted to meet you." There was something about him that was interesting to me. So my point is that I didn't connect with him through his music—I connected with him through his personality and his heart. I want my audience—even if I'm talking about something that isn't of interest to them that day—to think, "Well, let's see what she's going to say about it."

I interviewed Lady Gaga, whom I like a lot. I like her music and was smitten with her after being at a *Billboard* women's luncheon where she stood up and spoke to her parents about what they meant to her. As she talked, I thought, "Oh my God. She's so different from my perception of her. First, she's smart. She's deeper than people realize, and she has an interesting relationship with her parents." She was almost brought to tears by talking about them. When you see this girl running around in her underwear, or in a meat costume, you think, "Weird." But there's so much more to her than that. When she came to the show, I greeted her in my underwear. I stood there in my Spanx and my fishnets because I'd seen her do the same when she was interviewed by Anderson Cooper. She greeted him in her underwear and said, "I just don't feel like wearing clothes." So when she walked onto the set, I announced, "I don't feel like wearing clothes." It was hilarious. There were some people who asked, "Are you sure you want to do that?" I said, "What are people going to say? They know I'm not crazy, so they're going to say, 'Oh, Gayle has a big sense of humor.'" I think life is to be enjoyed!

I used to think that everybody had someone they could count on, someone they knew who fully understood them, got them, wanted the best for them, and supported them. But now I realize that's not the case for everyone, and I think it's very sad. It's so important to have at least one person you know won't betray you, who cheers you on, who wants what's best for you. I can't stress how important that is. You know, Oprah used to have a T-shirt that said, "Husbands come and go but friends last forever." When she wore it, we cracked up. "Ha! Isn't that funny?" I was married at the time, but years later, when I was divorced, I realized that it wasn't just funny, it was also true. When you're deeply in sync with someone, you're not so conscious about making time for one another. It's just something that flows naturally. If you're lucky, you have at least one really good friend, and the truth of the matter is, you only need one. That one person soothes your soul. She can carry you through a multitude of life's hurdles. For me, it was my mother. We would talk every day about everything and nothing. I mean, your mother is the person who wants to hear every little niggling detail of your life, but in many respects, a good girlfriend does, too. She genuinely wants you to be great. Women have friendships that men don't have. We share and really care about each other in a different, more present way. We lift each other up. A man can watch his friend going through the worst of times, play golf with him, and never even ask, "How you doing, man?" or "What happened?"

It saddens me when women think there's not enough to go around, because there's more than enough. It's a big old pie, y'all. I believe that when *you're* good at what you do, it only makes *me* better. I don't feel lesser than or not as good. Your success, your happiness lifts me up, which is something a lot of women haven't learned. They're thinking, "Well, let me knock her out of the way because she's encroaching on my territory," as opposed to "Bring her in because she'll make all of us look good."

Living in today's world, when everything is captured 24-7 in social media with no accountability, is hard. I look at some of the things on TV today, and I can't help but feel that our society encourages people to be their worst possible selves, to be as disrespectful, obnoxious, and rude as they can possibly be—and rewards them for it. Yet when you talk to people, a lot of them feel the same way I do. In fact, I think most people are concerned—and it's not just older generations. Even young people are saying, "Wait a second." I believe that good manners and learning right from wrong start at home. You can always make the decision to say, "I'm not doing that. He can do that. She can do that, but I'm not doing that." For that reason, I can't totally blame the media. But at the same time, we don't have to bottom out first.

The other day, my son Will and I were talking about OWN and its philosophy, which is to live your best life and encourage others. He said, "Mom, it's going to be hard in today's world because people just don't want to hear that." I disagree. Will's just looking at what's going on in the world. He's looking at what's happening in society. His belief is that people don't want to hear that message, and my belief is that they do. They're just trying to figure out where to get it from. When you talk to people one-on-one, they'll tell you they're still searching. I think that most of us are works in progress and that most of us strive to be better people. I know that I am and do. I don't care who you are, what level you're at, everybody's a work in progress and trying to be better.

Patti LaBelle

Patti LaBelle is a Grammy Award winner who got her start in the early 1960s with the Bluebelles and launched her solo career in 1977. She is a member of the Grammy Hall of Fame and in 2011 received a Lifetime Achievement Award at the BET Awards.

✦

Throughout my life, I've been inspired by tragedy and pain. I know tragedy and pain are not usually thought of as inspiring, but looking back, they were for me. I always say everything happens for a reason and that there's a lesson to be learned in every situation. When I was growing up in Philadelphia, my parents would fight a lot, which was rough for me. It inspired me not to have a relationship like theirs when I married. My mother and father did the best they could, and they were great with the kids, but they didn't treat each other well. I think I had a dysfunctional family growing up so it would make me work hard at not having one later on. The experience taught me to treat everyone with respect.

Despite their problems, my family has always been supportive of my singing. I remember the first time I discovered that I had a voice. I was about seven years old, and I started singing in front of the mirror with the broom as my microphone. And I was just killing it! I told myself, "Girl, you can sing!" I didn't really know what singing was, but I thought I had it.

Shortly after that, I started singing in the choir. For years the choir director tried to get me to do a solo. I told her, "No, I belong here in the back. I have no business singing lead." Eventually, she forced me to sing a duet with her son, and we just killed it. The entire church loved it. It was at that moment that I realized I should be singing for people. My mother and father also saw in that moment that I had a talent for singing. From then on, my whole family encouraged me, and that's when I got my first manager — in my early teenage years.

To this day, my biggest musical influence was my choir director, Mrs. Harriet Chatman, because she sang and played the piano so well. She's the one who encouraged me to be a better singer, and she taught me a lot. Kenny Gamble was my second-biggest influence. We grew up together. He knew I had a special gift, and he became my protector, keeping the neighborhood boys away so I could concentrate! Of course, this was before Philadelphia International Records, his now-famous label. Kenny nurtured me musically until he could record me.

Cindy Birdsong and I started our first group, called the Ordettes, when we were just teenagers. We weren't fabulous, but we were good enough. We didn't last that long, and after we broke up, our manager at the time introduced us to Nona Hendryx and Sarah Dash, which marked the beginning of Patti LaBelle and the Bluebelles.

It was challenging at first because of the times and how black women were treated. I didn't look like your typical lead singer. We'd hired a racist new manager, Harold Robinson. He didn't like the way I looked and really wasn't even interested in hearing me sing. He said, "You got that big nose, you're black, and you're ugly." I said, "I'm not ugly. I just have a big nose." And then we started to sing, and I blew him away. I guess he saw the green dollars coming out of that big ugly nose. Ironically, he was the one who gave me the name LaBelle, which means "the beauty." I said, "How can you give me that name if I'm ugly?" I let my talent speak for itself. I always have, and the rest is history!

I never thought of stardom. I wasn't motivated by a desire to be a star. I always just wanted to get onstage and show people how good I was. It was purely about singing. I think I can attribute my longevity — fifty-plus years in this business — to my singular desire to sing. I give my audiences a pure show every time I go onstage. One hundred fifty percent! My audiences know what they're going to get whenever they come to see Patti LaBelle.

One of the biggest moments in my career came in 1974. We'd been traveling around and performing everywhere, so I told our manager to book us at the Metropolitan Opera House in New York City. At first she didn't want to do it, because she didn't think she *could* do it. We insisted, and after much effort, we were finally booked for the legendary "Silver Night at the Met." LaBelle became the first African American contemporary act booked at the Met. And baby, we killed it! We tore the house down, along with Cher and others. That night was definitely a major highlight of my career.

Beyond any performance or musical success, my most significant life accomplishment has been motherhood. We weren't necessarily trying to have a baby, but we sure weren't doing anything to prevent it either. My baby, Zuri, is the biggest reward in my life. And even better, he's turned out to be such a cool guy. I was always on the road, but thankfully I had a great husband, Armstead, who was at times both father and mother to our son. I made up for lost time when I came home. I didn't spoil him, but I gave him my time. That's all he ever wanted and needed.

I think I've continued to be blessed because I give a lot of myself to others. Sometimes people who didn't deserve it have burned me, but for the most part, it's been good. I remember when Oprah Winfrey first started in Baltimore. At the time, no one wanted to do her show. I was performing at a theater there, and she would come and beg me to do her show. So I said, "Yes!" I went on her show lots of times back then, even when I didn't have a record out or anything special to talk about. She's always remembered me for that and included me in things even when other folks had bigger names at the time.

A few years ago, Oprah asked me to do Maya Angelou's birthday party. They set me up in a beautiful cottage in the Florida Keys, and while I was waiting, I was watching Oprah's show on TV. Then there was a knock at the door, and it was Oprah. I was in my muumuu, with my legs kicked up, relaxing. I said to her, "Good, you're here! I need some stockings for tonight." Being that it was Maya Angelou, I wanted to be ladylike. She didn't have any stockings, but she left me a big check. She said, "This is just because you've always been a friend to me." That was a beautiful moment. I think it's because I did her show when nobody else wanted to do it.

And speaking of Oprah, the Legends Ball in 2005 was amazing. "The Young'uns and the Legends" was the theme. We all broke down crying at the luncheon. Next to me were Mariah Carey, Chaka Khan, Mary J. Blige, and Diana Ross. Diana Ross and

I really hadn't been talking for years, so I said to her, "I've never known why we don't speak." And she said, "I don't know why either." So we started talking, and still do. I think that day Halle Berry and Angela Bassett connected for the first time in years, too. This was the day that people—black women—who thought they didn't get along, came together and got along. Oprah brought together so many people at that Legends Ball.

The good news is that black women have come a long way. I'm not saying things are as they should be, but they're so much better. I think some black women are kicking butt. Beyoncé? You can't find any entertainer who's stronger than her. Mary J. Blige is phenomenal! Women are definitely taking over—and not just in music, but everywhere. Michelle Obama is influencing a generation. She is the kind of woman we'd all like to have as a girlfriend. There are many powerful women out there doing their thing and doing it well! I always try to support other black women because I definitely think the industry pits black women against each other. That's why it's important for Dionne Warwick, Gladys Knight, and me to do shows together. It doesn't matter who's first or last; it's the fact that we're onstage together.

I've never given up. I always keep going no matter what. My only advice to young women is never to make the same mistake twice and never to be shady in business. Shadiness in business may bring you short-term success, but it will always come back to haunt you. As they say, "What goes around, comes around," but I've messed up. If you make a big enough mistake and you've been given a second chance, you can't mess up and do it again. Grow and keep going, but like I said, try not to make the same mistake twice.

I'm blessed to still be doing this at sixty-six, but I don't feel that I've gotten over my rainbow yet. I still have hills to climb. I don't feel like I've completed what I've been put here to do. When people ask me if I consider myself an icon, I say, "Hell no! Not yet. Maybe after I do that next thing." I take it as a blessing that people think of me that way, but I'm still climbing. Each day I'm motivated by the fact that I know I can make somebody happy with my talent. I can still sing! I can still move! And I can still kick my shoes off! And hopefully I can be an inspiration to some young girl who says to herself, "If that old lady can do it, I know I can!"

Debra L. Lee

Debra L. Lee joined BET Networks, of which she is now chairwoman and CEO, after attending Brown University and Harvard Law School. She practiced law for six years and then joined BET's legal affairs department. She became president and COO in 1996 and CEO in 2005.

✳

My dad was a major in the U.S. Army, so we moved around a lot. I was born in South Carolina, at Fort Jackson, and then we were transferred to Germany, to D.C., and then to Los Angeles. Some of my fondest childhood memories are of seeing the world and making new friends.

My dad retired when I was in sixth grade, and we moved to Greensboro, North Carolina, which was still segregated at the time. I went to an all-black junior high school and an all-black high school. At both, we had teachers who really supported us and told us we could be anything we wanted to be. I was fortunate to have parents and teachers who believed in me. My parents were committed to providing us with the best education they could, and they instilled in us a sense of responsibility and of the importance of working hard at school. I remember my dad used to give me a dollar for every A that I received, which in those days was a big incentive to do well.

The sixties and early seventies were an exciting time to grow up. The country was in transition on many fronts. At my high school, we had "Save the Black Schools" days because we weren't convinced that integration was the way to resolve racial inequality. We believed that if we were allowed to compete, we'd be okay. We were proud of our school and our community; we were taught the value of good leadership and the importance of giving back. On the black side of town, we had our own lawyers, our own doctors, and our own bank, so we never wanted for much of anything. We believed we were special.

But just the same, we were aware of the need to "fit in." My first paying job was in Belk's department store, in the jewelry section. I had a big Afro at the time, and the lady who interviewed me for the position nicely asked, "Is there another way you can wear your hair?" I remember understanding what she was getting at right away: She wanted me to straighten my hair. She was like, "Okay, if this young woman straightens her hair, maybe people won't think about the fact that she's black. Maybe she'll blend in a little better." I understood. I straightened my hair, and I got the job.

I have been an avid reader as long as I can remember, and I have been keenly interested in the African American experiences depicted in literature and television from a very young age. When I was growing up, the book that made the biggest impression on me was *The Autobiography of Malcolm X*. I remember sitting on our front stoop reading it, and my father telling me I wasn't old enough to read it. Of course, I read it anyway. I was struck by the many different phases of transformation and enlightenment in Malcolm X's life.

There wasn't a whole lot of TV to watch, but I remember *The Ed Sullivan Show* and the excitement in our household if the Supremes or the Temptations made an appearance. It was always a big event if there was a black person on television—whether it was Diahann Carroll on *Julia* or someone else on *The Flip Wilson Show* or *The Nat "King" Cole Show*. Everyone would call each other up to let each other know. It was the days of Motown, and besides the Supremes and the Temptations, among my many role models was Stevie Wonder.

My dad wanted me to go to an Ivy League school, to take advantage of the educational opportunities that were opening up for African American students. When I look back, I realize that it sometimes felt like a burden to be among the first generation of African Americans to have these kinds of opportunities—the expectations for us could be overwhelming. One of my biggest breaks was going to Harvard Law School. I won't ever downplay what an amazing experience it was. Just the people I met and the opportunities I have had as a result—I'll wear that on my sleeve no matter where

I go. No one can ever take it away. I mean, look at our first black president. Where did he go to school? Harvard Law School!

I tell young people to pursue something they're passionate about because if they're really going to be the best at whatever it is they do, they have got to work really hard at it. They have got to devote most of their time to it and understand that it will affect their personal lives. If it's something you love, it makes things easier. Then I remind them to be flexible. Often success lies in your ability to take advantage of opportunities that arise, whether they're expected or not, and a willingness to work your way up. I remember I was a receptionist at a law firm one summer and it was pretty monotonous, but I took away that you have to work really hard before reaching whatever your ultimate goals may be. You can't expect just to step into the perfect job, the perfect career. You have to pay your dues, do some grunt work—something that young people don't understand these days. They come into a company, and after six months they want to know about their promotion. I'm like, "Well, it doesn't really happen that fast." Or they're asking for a raise. That's another thing that I tell young people: "Don't always expect a raise when you take on new responsibilities. Eventually, you'll get one, but you have got to consider the value of the experience first." When I joined BET, I was general counsel, but I also had business responsibilities. I learned about the company by being willing to take on anything.

A couple of years ago, I took a survey about values, and I realized that one of my values—I think I got this from my parents—is achievement. I like achieving things. I like setting goals and accomplishing them. The great thing about business is that every day you have goals: You have annual goals, you have monthly goals, and in television, you have daily goals based on ratings. The next challenge is what keeps me going. My vision is to produce great original content. Part of getting there is putting together the right team, hiring great programmers and producers. I want BET to be the first place that African Americans with projects think to approach. I want them to take pride in having their shows on BET, in knowing that we make a special connection with our audience.

I'm also inspired by running a black business and proving to the world that African Americans can do things as well as anyone else. People at BET take that very seriously. We want to beat everybody—whether it's MTV, NBC, or whatever. To be able to work at a company aimed at African Americans and to be able to accomplish my goals within that company is still incredibly motivating to me.

Today I look up to Dr. Ruth Simmons, who is the president of Brown University. She has a great head on her shoulders and has been a wonderful role model. I'm on the Board of Trustees of Brown, so I have had the chance to watch her work. I have always looked up to politicians and lawyers because that's where I started my career. Whether it's Constance Baker Motley or someone like Congresswoman Maxine Waters, many of my role models come from the legal and political worlds. It can be hard to find female role models in these industries. There just haven't been a lot of women in top positions, which is why I take it very seriously when a young woman tells me, "I look up to you." It really means a lot to me. It's a wonderful thing to inspire someone.

I consider myself lucky to have witnessed the first African American president and first family. It's exciting to know the president and First Lady, to be near the seat of power. It's an incredible time to be in Washington. I have power within my industry, and it's great to be in a position to be able to work with the Obama administration to make a difference.

I'm passionate about my own children, and really all children, about making sure they get a good start in life, and about my community and African Americans in general. I'm passionate about the media industry and the positive impact it can have on our community, the way it can give back and inspire people, especially young people. I have always liked being a mentor and trying to help those coming up behind me. What I do at BET is a way to do just that: to spread information, to give advice, to set expectations, to put forth positive role models for our kids, and to shape the images of men and women of color. I'm proud of the quality of our original programming and of our ability to be competitive within our industry. I'm happy to be at a place in my life where I can give back. I have a lot of optimism about what we can accomplish, about the economy, and about the future in general.

Soledad O'Brien

Soledad O'Brien hosts CNN's In America *documentary series. She is the mother of four children and the author of* The Next Big Story: My Journey Through the Land of Possibilities.

✳

I grew up in a very tight family. Part of that was because we were pretty much the only minority family in our community of St. James, New York. My mother is African Cuban and my father is Australian Irish. So, on the one hand, we didn't really fit in, but on the other, since we had a big family, it didn't really matter. I always had brothers and sisters to play with. My mom had six kids in seven years, so we were close in age as well as emotionally. We always had dinner together. It was classic — every night, everyone around the table. As my brothers and sisters got older, and the older ones were getting ready to go to college, they became more argumentative, especially in terms of intellectual conversations at dinner. And that's really where I learned to argue and to make my point. I had to take a side and defend my idea, whether it was about a movie I liked or didn't like, or something else.

When I was growing up, my parents were heroic characters to me. They built a life, and I looked up to them and tried to model my life after theirs. Both of my parents are educators, and they're obsessed with education. Truly obsessed. Their mantra has always been "You have to be educated." I think part of that is the immigrant mentality, the idea that an education is something no one can take away from you. Once you have your education, no matter where you go, no matter what happens, no matter what your circumstances, you will have a degree from X. And so they were very aggressive about education. It wasn't like, "You all need to go to Harvard" — although we all ended up there in some capacity. They absolutely, positively had no specific academic agenda for any of us. But what they did want was for us to be kind and generous people, and they wanted us to be happy. Those were their goals.

My parents are also very religious, very devout. So that meant church every Sunday. It also meant that my brothers and sisters and I were the first to leave parties. For the most part, we didn't do much besides study and go to school, but we were allowed to watch as much news as we wanted. At that time, there was *The MacNeil/Lehrer Report*, which I loved. I always thought it would be great to be a reporter on the show. Desperately, to this day, it's my dream job to work with Jim Lehrer because I'm secretly in love with him. I really ended up learning a lot from the news about what was going on in the world, more than, "Oh, this is what I want to be when I grow up." I never really thought much about that. But I did think, "Oh, there's a big world out there of interesting things that are happening."

In a way, I didn't have any real challenges growing up. I had a very middle-class existence, but I was constantly being reminded by other people that I didn't quite fit in. I remember I was invited to one girl's house, a classmate I thought was my best friend in eighth grade, and her sister complained at the dinner table, "I don't want to sit next to the black girl." And I was like, "Oh, huh," because clearly they'd been having conversations about "the black girl." Or people just wouldn't invite me over. It was typical eighth grader behavior in a certain way, but sometimes there was a racial tinge to it that was unpleasant and uncomfortable. It reminded me that everyone didn't see me the way I saw myself, which was as fitting in nicely.

I really discovered that I loved words when I got to Harvard. I already knew that I loved to write. I enjoyed the process, and I wanted to be an English literature major, no matter what. I loved capturing what a person was trying to say, getting it exactly right, with all the nuances. Working as a journalist in the newsroom, I've learned from people who are absolutely, pathologically obsessed with accuracy, which has made me absolutely, pathologically obsessed with it also. One of the biggest upsides of my job is that I get to meet the people who inspire me the most and borrow from them. I worked with Katie Couric when I was at *Today*, and we are friends to this day. She's amazing.

Being the first is never easy, and she did it with incredible grace—even under attack. I would watch her and watch the barbs and think, "I can't believe she's not snapping." She got out there every day and knocked out a good show, even as the critics were poised with their pens to write evil things. And what did she do? She got back out there and won award after award for the best newscast. I think that's incredibly inspiring. I've learned so much from watching Katie's career unfold.

I want to empower young women to take control of the opportunities in their lives. Most of the girls I mentor come out of poverty and have had either very challenging economic circumstances or really tough situations at home. My message to them is "Look how far you've come. Use the strength you already have. I didn't help you get here. I was not there while you were doing your homework. I didn't call your teachers. You've come so far on your own. That's an incredible strength and an incredible power. You need to harness it, and in doing so, you can be wildly successful because you've already been wildly successful. I'm here to help you through the gap."

I think my longevity in this business is attributable to flexibility. Flexibility is everything, and I've never minded change. It's part of what makes a good reporter. My schedule is never set, so I have to stay open; I can't possibly get all the things done that I need to get done. I've had ups and downs in my career, but I've always welcomed change. That attitude has really helped me because every project I've been assigned, everything I've moved on to do, has always seemed like a really exciting opportunity. For example, when I was taken off *American Morning*, I started doing documentaries, something I hadn't really done before. My first one was *Black in America*, and it was a massive success. I've always felt that every single time something challenging has happened, it's turned out to be an amazing opportunity. It's opened the door to doing something I would never have had the chance to do otherwise. Flexibility has allowed me to eke out the best in any situation.

My kids grew up on the set, so they have a good idea of what I do. When a story breaks, they know that Mom travels. That's what I do. I remember going to Haiti. I couldn't get in at first because it was nearly impossible to get a flight. A few people were choppering in, but I couldn't get on a chopper. Finally, my daughter Sophia said,

"Somebody better send Mommy to Haiti. There will be no rest until Mommy gets to Haiti!"

When I started covering New Orleans after Hurricane Katrina, I fell in love with the city, and I still spend a lot of time there now. Was it the most important story of our time? No. But it was a big story at the time, because so many questions about race and accountability, the underclass and poverty, responsibility for your citizens, and citizens' responsibility for their neighbors came to light. It wasn't just about New Orleans. It was about what happens to an American city when there's a disaster. Do people abandon it or do they step up to save it? And guess what? They have to save themselves at the same time. New Orleans is a metaphor for any place that has a natural disaster. When I cover a story, I don't think of it in big, broad brushstrokes. I think of it in the moment. What is the most important aspect of the story, and how can I help CNN in telling it? What's my part in it, and how do I do that well? That's really my focus.

I'm a glass-half-full kind of person. I don't live in the world of regrets, in part because who knows if something I regret might have made all the difference in how I got to where I am now. I feel I've had a really good career. Good in that I've had wonderful opportunities and I've produced great work. I think my work has value and is valued. It's been critically acclaimed, and I like it. I'm entertained by what I do. I think it matters when I run out the door, rolling my little suitcase behind me. It matters that I'm getting on the plane because I've got an important interview to do, an interview that only I can do—or that only I can do in a certain way. That's all you can ask from a career. And I have four healthy, happy kids and a husband I love. I feel very blessed on all fronts.

Keke Palmer

Keke Palmer is a child actress and singer. She stars on Nickelodeon's True Jackson, VP *and received acclaim for her work in 2006's* Akeelah and the Bee.

✶

The most important values my mom and dad instilled in me are a belief in myself, humility, and a respect for other people. They also taught me to be giving, to remain true to who I am, and to have a good relationship with God. My parents have been married for twenty-three years. They met in a theater class in college in Chicago and dated for two years. My mom told me they were inseparable and decided to get married before they graduated. My family is extremely close, and we really depend on each other. When we first moved to California from Chicago for my acting career, all we had was each other—my mother, father, sisters, brother, and me.

I started singing in church at a very young age, so everybody knew early on that I could sing. What they didn't know was that I also could act. They just knew I had an outgoing personality. Even when I was a small child, people would say, "Keke should be a singer or on TV," but you hear stuff like that all the time. When I was nine and a half years old, my mom took me to an audition for the Broadway production of *The Lion King.* Out of four hundred kids, I made it to the top fifteen finalists. That was my first introduction to acting. From the start, I thought it was so cool: I was meeting all these new people, and I loved going to auditions and competing. It was all new and fresh and fun. When my mom truly realized how much I loved it, she said, "Let's go for it and really do this!" That's when my family decided to move to the West Coast. Of course, it was a difficult decision because we were leaving the world we knew for the unknown. But we just prayed and asked God to pave the way. We packed up, and the whole family drove four days and three nights to California.

I consider my first real big break in the entertainment business to be a TV movie I did with William H. Macy called *The Wool Cap*, which is about a mute man who's the superintendent of an apartment building and a little girl who lives there with her mother, who's on drugs. The mother leaves the daughter in the super's care when she goes to pay off some of her debt. It's a story of an unlikely friendship and how two people grow to really care for one another. I earned a Screen Actors Guild nomination and was the youngest person ever to be nominated for the award in a lead actress role.

Despite the critical success of *The Wool Cap*, my phone didn't exactly ring off the hook afterward, because there just aren't many roles for young black girls. But then I found out about a new movie being cast called *Akeelah and the Bee*, and I immediately auditioned for the part of Akeelah. There were thousands of young girls at the open casting call, but I tried to keep that out of my head. My mom taught me at a young age not to compete with anybody. She would always use the example of Michael Jackson, who never competed with anybody other than himself. He wasn't distracted by what anyone else was doing. Instead, he focused on what he was doing and on trying to better himself. My mom wanted me to concern myself only with me and with topping what I'd done.

My mom was really good at making auditioning fun. When I was younger, it wouldn't matter how interesting a script was because I was too little to even grasp the story, which would have been boring to me anyway. So my mom came up with the idea of involving the whole family. We would table-read at home, with my dad, my older sister, my mom, and me all going through the script together. In that way I saw the story in its true colors, instead of as a bunch of words written on a piece of paper. It really helped me understand what I was doing and was an excellent way for me to prepare for auditions.

I auditioned about six or seven times for *Akeelah and the Bee* before I was offered the part. After every audition I'd tell my mom, "I'm going to get the part," and it wasn't in an arrogant way. I've always said that God gave me the gift of perception and that I can feel things. I've always been able to tell if I've done a great job at an audition or if they didn't want me, which is okay, too. I always remind myself, "Keke, you did your best and you did a great job, but if they don't select you, then you're not what they were looking for." But throughout the *Akeelah and the Bee* process, I just knew in my heart that I'd get the part. I've always been good at being able to read people. Sometimes casting directors have been stone-faced, but most of the time I've just known what they felt about my performance. When I told my mom what I felt after the *Akeelah and the Bee* audition, she said, "Keke, don't say that. You did your best and that's all. Now just walk away from it." But I knew after my last audition—when I did that crying scene—I just knew it. I still joke about when I was leaving the room and the director, Doug Atchison, told me, "Thank you so much." I knew his intent was to thank me for making it easy to give me the part. I swear that's what his mind was saying to me. I was only eleven years old at the time, but after I got the part, I told him exactly what I'd been thinking.

After *Akeelah and the Bee* came out, I felt a bunch of different emotions. People had set up the movie to be so big in my mind. They'd say, "You're going to be huge. You're going to be everywhere." My mom told me not to pay attention to that stuff, because it might not come true. People might not care about the movie. Because of the big buildup, I had great expectations, but *Akeelah* turned out to be more of a sleeper hit than an overnight box-office success. A lot of teachers have shown the DVD and discussed it with their classes. So it did well a year or so after it was released, but not right away. People thought it was going to be a boring film about a spelling bee, but in reality the spelling bee was just a backdrop. The film is really about believing in yourself and not letting your community tell you who you should be. It's about knowing you can be far bigger than anything surrounding you, and the idea that it's all up to you. If you believe in yourself, anything is possible, as long as you try your very best. That's the message of the film, and it speaks to you if you're an adult or a kid. We've all been in situations where we've felt like we couldn't achieve something. We've all felt like "I'm not going to succeed" or "I haven't gone to such and such college, so I can't achieve this or that." Now, years later, all different kinds of people—white, black, adults, kids—come up to me and want to talk about *Akeelah*, and I've come to realize that I really did accomplish what I wanted to, which was for many people to see the movie and get its message.

As for balancing acting and singing, I've been able to do both with lots of hard work. I signed with Atlantic Records when I was twelve years old, and I did a song on the *Akeelah and the Bee* soundtrack called "All My Girlz." I left Atlantic a year later to sign with Interscope Records, which is when I also began to realize that a lot of kids my age really didn't know me. My manager at the time told me about a new television show called *True Jackson, VP*, which was coming out on Nickelodeon. I thought if I got this TV show, I'd be closer to my peers, which would keep me relevant. They'd see me and know me through the show, and with my new album coming out, they'd have another way to reach me. I especially hoped to accomplish all this with *True Jackson, VP* because it was a really good show with such positive images. It puts not only young girls, but also African Americans, in a good light.

True Jackson has inspired young people to think, "I can do anything no matter what my age or my color. I can do anything I want to do as long as I push myself, work hard, and stay focused." And that's why I wanted to do the show. The producers were looking for all types of girls: black, white, Latina, Asian. They wanted the right person, regardless of color, and I'm the type of person who'll go out for any role, whether it's supposed to be a black or a white character. Recently, I auditioned for a role that's specifically white, but that didn't stop me. Look at someone like Whoopi Goldberg. Many of the roles she's known for were not written for an African American person. Even her part in *Sister Act* was originally written for Bette Midler. Whenever I think about that, I tell people that it doesn't matter whom the role's intended for. If you're interested in it, go audition for it!

On a scale from one to ten, I'd say my confidence is between eight and a half and nine and a half! I get my self-assurance from my mom and from God, because I always trust that I'll get what's meant for me. If I don't end up getting the part or the job, then it wasn't meant for me and I can walk away from it. I don't feel like "Oh my goodness, I'm devastated," because I know that God didn't want it for me.

Some of my main challenges have been in music because I've grown accustomed to reaching so many different ages and so many different races with my film and television work. With music it can be more cut-and-dried, and the industry doesn't always know what to do with a person like me. I can't do just R&B music or just pop music, because if I only did one straight style, then I'd be leaving out people. If I wanted to do only urban music, I'd leave out the pop fans; if I only wanted to do pop music, I'd leave out my urban fans. People in the industry are accustomed to saying, "Okay, you're black, so go to urban," or, "You're white, so go to pop," and that's not me. That confuses people. Also, because I'm already known, they don't want to mess up a brand that's established. But I'm happy right now, and I think Interscope is the best label for me. I see my music as simple to categorize: pop R&B. I'd say what I do is similar to Whitney Houston, because she's also internationally loved by every race and every age.

I'm so inspired by my mom—who she is as a person and with everything that she's done for me and my siblings. I'm also inspired by Will Smith and Queen Latifah. I just love how they have created their own empires. They started out as rappers, doing something that can seem so stereotypical to the masses, but then they expanded on it. They became entrepreneurs. They became their own businesses; they make their own films, and they manage other people. They're incredibly impressive! Will Smith and Queen Latifah are blessed with good genes, an understanding of the importance of trial and error, and focus. I remember Queen Latifah telling me that the people she works with now are the same people she went to high school with. Back then, they had their own little crew, and their plan was to get into the entertainment industry and make things happen. They just believed in themselves and went for it. Their drive is so inspiring to me.

I always tell young girls to stay true to themselves and not to change or compromise their morals. Along the way, a lot of people have tried to make me compromise my sense of what's right. You can't let yourself get consumed by the money or let anyone tell you, "This is what you have to do." You can't let those things affect you. You have to try to keep your head on straight and remember what you had before you got deep into the business. I feel a tremendous obligation to the young people who are watching me, because I know kids are impressionable, and I understand that with much privilege comes much responsibility. I also want to be a good example to my little brother and sister, who are watching me very closely.

I think my ability to transition from child actor to young adult actor lies in not settling for just any role. I've been very selective. It's all about the quality of the work, and I was blessed very early on in my career with quality roles, which set up an automatic standard for me. Even though I want to work all the time, I won't take on a role unless it moves me in some authentic way. It has to provoke real emotion, like make me laugh out loud, or cry, or even make me angry—if I feel an emotion, then I want to do the role. This way of choosing roles sets me apart from a lot of young actors who aren't as selective.

The best thing about my life is that I'm genuinely happy. Yes, I have bad times like everyone else. But I thank God for being happy, because there are people who are unhappy in every form and every way, no matter how good their lives are. I'm so grateful that I wake up and I'm in a good mood and in a good place in my heart and my mind. I'm happy that my spirit's doing well. That's such a blessing. In my life and career, I'd like to change the world. I sing, I dance, and I act. I have a lot on the horizon that I'm really proud of and excited about. I want to change people's minds and get them to understand that you can do it all. And I want to do it all at the highest level that I possibly can. I want people to look at what I'm doing and say, "Wow!" I want to inspire people. Whenever you have done something and people come along and try to do it better than you because they have seen what you're capable of doing, then they grow, too. I want to be able to do that for my generation. I don't want to be just okay in life, I want to be great.

Tracy Reese

Tracy Reese is a fashion designer and graduate of the Parsons School of Design. She launched her eponymous collection in 1996 and introduced her lower-priced line, Plenty by Tracy Reese, in 1997. In 2007 Ms. Reese was inducted as a board member of the Council of Fashion Designers of America.

✳

I was very fortunate as a child. I grew up on the northwest side of Detroit. I had great parents and a wonderful extended family, from my aunts and uncles to really strong grandmothers. Your family shapes you. Our parents weren't wealthy by any means—we were a normal middle-class family—but we were never held back from doing anything we really wanted to do. They always found a way for us to take classes, to have meaningful experiences, to go to camp. We were brought up in a traditional way. Our parents were strict: We didn't get away with anything, we didn't curse, we didn't talk back—classic black family stuff.

Things weren't given to us flat out. We had to work for them. Like, if we wanted a particular kind of clothing, we had to earn the money to buy it ourselves. I think a lot of that mentality is getting lost as time goes on. All parents want to provide as well as they can for their kids, but you also have to help them provide for themselves when they can. That's how you prepare them to be out in the world. For my parents, it was always important that we contribute in whatever little way we could, whether it was by doing chores around the house, babysitting, or shoveling snow. When I was in high school, I had a few jobs. I worked in a restaurant and then in a fabric store called Pearl's House of Fine Fabrics. As a kid, I loved having my own money, and I believe that a sense of self-sufficiency is an important thing to instill in young people.

My mom always sewed, and when I was ten, she taught me. My mother and I would make outfits together, shop in the pattern books, go out to buy fabric—the whole deal. We used to have sewing parties in the basement. All I needed to know was that the Ebony Fashion Fair Show was coming to town, and there was the incentive to make a new outfit.

My mom was a big believer in keeping busy on the weekends. There was great emphasis on not being lazy, on not allowing ourselves to be bored. After we completed our chores on Saturdays, we went off to classes. I had swimming or art; my sister Leslie had dance; and my other sister, Erin, had gymnastics. We all had something to do on Saturdays.

When I got to Cass Technical High School, the head of the art department convinced me to take drawing classes. I signed up for model drawing, fashion design, and figure drawing. The fashion design department at Cass was headed by Dr. Cledie Taylor, an amazing woman. If she thought any of us were serious, she'd say, "You know, you should consider going to Parsons for college. It's the best fashion education you can get, and they're always interested in really good students." Through Dr. Taylor and her successor, Marion Stevens, I applied for the Parsons summer program for high school students, and I got a scholarship for the tuition. I came to New York and stayed with my aunt and uncle in New Jersey. They had two fresh babies—one eleven months old and one newborn, which was fabulous. I was able to help them out and take classes in the city. That summer, I took model drawing, design, and some kind of draping class.

The Parsons program was an eye-opener. When I was younger, sewing with my mom, I thought of fashion as a hobby, like sketching. At Parsons, I discovered that it could be a career. I hadn't realized what a big industry it is, the many facets of the business. I was like, "You know what? This is for me!" So I went back to Parsons for college and got a great education. I worked superhard with long hours, lots of classes, and lots of homework. I finished the program in three years, in part because of my training at Cass. I was able to skip freshman foundation because my high school art classes had been so strong.

I've been designing professionally since 1984. I haven't had one big break, but more a series of little ones. Tracy Reese has always had slow and constant growth. There was a moment when we had just started dealing with a lot of department stores, and then the business grew more swiftly, but for the most part, it's happened more gradually and in stages.

Constantly improving and striving to do better is what drives me. The fashion industry is perfectly set up for that mentality, because we have many seasons, more than are publicized. We actually have ten deliveries. We deliver ten months out of twelve, and we're always trying to do things better. I look at whatever we did last season like, "Okay, this was good, but it would have been better if we'd done this or that." Or, "Customers need more of this or that. Let's see how we can work it in, update it, and keep it new." There's a constant challenge to improve upon what we're doing, to make it more beautiful, more accessible, and more affordable. It's an opportunity to better myself, ten times a year. There are so many layers to consider when you're creating clothes—from designing them and choosing the colors and textures of the fabrics, to making them and coming up with pieces that work in a way that's exciting.

It's a funny process with retail and fashion. There are things we design that I love but that sell poorly. Then there are things that I'm not satisfied with that sell well. It's difficult to predict what will be a hit. Sometimes it comes from left field, when I'm not expecting it at all. Because we're showing clothes that people won't be buying for another eight or nine months—sometimes up to a year—I have to remain open, keep my ear to the ground, and do my best to anticipate.

I attribute my longevity in this business to my desire to stay in the game. I think a lot of people give up because the combination of elements can be tough. Sometimes

I ask myself, "Is this worth everything I'm putting into it? Am I getting enough out of it?" And that's not necessarily from a financial standpoint. It's a heart thing, too. Like, "I'm putting all this into it. Does this customer even want me to put all this into it?" Everybody's different. I've seen some people throw in the towel after having a good business, because the market can be so brutal.

One of our biggest challenges came when we first started. We were doing production in India and hired people there to work for us. We did our best to monitor the quality. I traveled back and forth, almost five times a year, to work with them on fit and finishing garments. But after about ten years, I realized things weren't getting better fast enough so we had to pull out. That was a huge disappointment. It was tough to give up, because there's so much potential in that country, but it was difficult to marry that potential with the business acumen needed to produce good-quality clothing on time. You know, anybody can do it if you give them all the time in the world, but we're on a tight schedule. It was difficult for them to be competitive producers for that reason, which was sad on both sides.

For every challenge, there's some wonderful thing that makes me want to go to work every day. I'm inspired by so much. Good art, travel, being in a beautiful setting. Color in a general sense inspires me, specifically color from nature, but sometimes synthetic colors, too. Fabric inspires me. The way certain people dress inspires me. I love watching old movies. I love a lot of designers from the past, especially from the 1920s. I love furniture and interiors. There's inspiration everywhere you look; it just depends on where you're focused.

I'm passionate about creating things, so I get really bummed postshow. The letdown is huge after a show because I'm physically exhausted and the thing that's been driving me for the past several months has come to an end. Fortunately, that feeling only lasts a couple of days because by then I'm already late with the next thing!

The most exciting part of my work is seeing people wearing my clothes. I see somebody on the street or at an event, and they're wearing something I designed, and it looks good. That's really rewarding. I mean, it's great to see the models in my clothes. Of course that's fun, but to see real women in them is even more gratifying. And when

Michelle Obama wore one of my dresses on the cover of *People* magazine, I was just like, "Wow! Wow! What could be better?" It was amazing for me as a designer and amazing for us as a company. It was such a gift.

I tell young people who want to start their own fashion design business that it's going to be a lot of hard work, a lot of long hours—not nine to five by any stretch of the imagination. They need to know that they're responsible for their product, from conception to somebody wearing it and beyond. We've gotten calls about damage to a garment that's four years old. What do you do about that? They should also know that they're not just designing for themselves. It's not a selfish occupation. If they expect to have a customer, they have to put her first. They need to get a good education, go to the very best school they can get into and afford. And then they need to spend time working for someone else so they get experience and make some money before striking out on their own.

I still don't feel like I've arrived. I'm doing what I love to do, but I think we can do and be so much more. I may never feel that I've made it, and maybe I shouldn't. I think maybe that's a dangerous feeling. I don't want to become complacent. I want to keep trying and to enjoy the journey. I'm proud that I built this company. While it's definitely nice for my name to be inside of my clothing, it's more important that it stands for something—something that's good and of quality.

Shonda Rhimes

Shonda Rhimes is a TV producer and the creator of Grey's Anatomy *and* Private Practice. *She is a graduate of Dartmouth College and the University of Southern California's School of Cinema-Television. Ms. Rhimes has received multiple Image Awards for her writing, and in 2007, along with the women of* Grey's Anatomy, *she won the Lucy Award for Women in Film.*

*

I grew up in the south suburbs of Chicago. I came from a big, close-knit family and have five older brothers and sisters. My parents were intellectuals and spent most of their time reading or discussing art, literature, or politics. Education was extremely important to them. In our household when I was growing up, there was a lot of spirited debate and discussion, and books were considered a part of the family. I always joke that I lived in Chicago but I grew up in books. My mother had an amazing rule, which was that I could read whatever I wanted. She never censored anything, so I read everything. I read the *The French Lieutenant's Woman* when I was eight. My favorite book when I was younger was probably *To Kill a Mockingbird* or *The Color Purple*. It was great for someone like me, with a creative mind, to have the freedom to pull any book I wanted off the shelf. It worked, and it fostered my love of reading.

Our household was warm and traditional. When I was young, my mother was at home for the most part, and my dad went to work. When I got older, my mother went back to school—first to college, and then I watched her get her PhD. I went to a small Catholic school called St. Mary's. Ms. Hanks, my teacher from fifth grade through eighth, was my favorite teacher when I was growing up because she never talked down to us. She talked to us like we were adults. She was a very influential teacher.

My mother was a teacher, as was my sister, and I consider teaching to be a great profession. A good teacher can move mountains, while a bad teacher can destroy dreams.

I went to Dartmouth College in New Hampshire, where I majored in English literature and creative writing. Though I was two credits shy of being a double major in drama or art history, I always knew I was going to be an English major. When I graduated, I spent a year in San Francisco, working for an advertising agency and trying to figure out what I wanted to do with my life. My parents felt strongly that I should get a PhD in something, or go to law school or medical school, but I knew I wanted to be a writer. Only I was afraid that writing wasn't a real job. Then I read in the *New York Times* that it was harder to get into USC's School of Cinematic Arts than into Harvard Law School. I've always been the kind of person who went after whatever was considered impossible or difficult or really competitive, so I applied. When I got in, I went.

I was in the master of fine arts screenwriting program, which consists mainly of classes in production, editing, and writing, but I studied all aspects of filmmaking. While I was a student, two things happened. The first was that I'd written a thesis script called *When Willows Touch*. The story is set in the South in the 1930s and centers on a black family and their field of corn. There are dead bodies rotting in the corn. The father refuses to bury the bodies, and you discover why. It's a dark and twisted tale, but it got me an agent. The second thing that happened when I was a student was that I got an internship at Denzel Washington's company, Mundy Lane Entertainment. At that time, the company was run by Debra Martin Chase. She didn't like to do coverage, so I would read the scripts, and rather than write reports, I would talk to her about them. We developed a great relationship in the process and got to know each other.

After I graduated, Debra helped me get my first job, which was working as an assistant at Paula Weinstein's company, Spring Creek Productions. I worked there for about a year, until I realized that as long as I was working at a production company, I would never have time to write. I was too busy reading other people's scripts, working, and thinking about other things. I left to take a job as an administrative assistant outside the industry. I worked for an organization called Portals, which helps the mentally ill and homeless learn job skills and find places to live. It was a difficult job, but it was nine to five. At five o'clock, I could put down whatever I was doing, go home, and write. It wasn't a job that I loved, it wasn't my passion, but it allowed me to write.

To me, if I wasn't writing every day, I wasn't a writer. Eventually I told myself, "You have to finish something or sell something, or else you have to leave L.A. You're a very talented, very smart, and very together woman. You cannot be an administrative assistant for the rest of your life." That's what drove me. I wrote a spec script, a romantic comedy called *Human Seeking Same.* It was about an older white woman who falls in love with a younger black man when she answers the wrong personal ad. I gave it to my agent, and he put it on the spec market. My plan was that if the script sold, I'd stay in California, and if it didn't, I'd go back east to graduate school of some kind. It sold in twenty-four hours, so I stayed.

My first big break was selling that script. It wasn't made into a film, but it was put in turnaround twice, so I got paid for it twice. The spec market was very hot at the time and many movies didn't get made, but that script was my entrée into the industry. After it sold, lots of doors opened. I started to get writing jobs, like the HBO movie *Introducing Dorothy Dandridge.* Debra also did a lot for me. She hired me to be the research director on the documentary *Hank Aaron: Chasing the Dream*, which was nominated for an Oscar. Selling my first script meant that I was paid to be a writer, that I could stay in L.A. and make a living doing what I wanted to do.

I was doing films and rewrites on movies, which was all fine and great. I was enjoying myself. Then I started writing some teen girl movies. I rewrote every teen girl movie in town. It was a lovely living, but I was in that place that most people get to in their early thirties where I was just a little sick of myself, sick of my life. I was absolutely, totally navel-gazing in the most ridiculous thirty-year-old way. I wondered, "Where am I going? What am I doing? What does life mean?" So I rented this big house in Vermont. My plan was to live there and write for a month and figure myself out. It seems so silly now, but I got on a plane and went to Vermont. I moved into this giant farmhouse in the middle of nowhere, and the next day, 9/11 happened. There I was, watching on satellite TV the most horrible images I'd ever seen in my life. I remember asking myself, "If the world ends tomorrow, what have you done? What is it that you really want to do? You had better start living because you're not going to live forever." So I decided to adopt a baby. The idea probably came from every book I ever read as a kid. I always thought I'd adopt a child. When I got back to L.A. from Vermont, I hired an adoption attorney, and nine months and two days after 9/11, my daughter was born. At thirty-one, I became a single mom.

Overnight, I went from going out every night with friends to being home every night with a baby. I quickly discovered that it's a lot harder to go out if you have a

child. Your whole life really does change. I found myself up at night with my daughter at my chest, watching television, which I'd never really done before. I discovered that television is where all the really good character development happens. Part of my malaise with regard to the movie industry was that everything has to be solved in two hours maximum, which is never that exciting. But in television, characters can grow and change and be really complex. I remember that I watched all seven seasons of *Buffy the Vampire Slayer* in like a week and an entire season of *24* in twenty-four hours. I discovered *The Sopranos* and some other really amazing stuff.

After watching all this television, I went to my agent and said, "I think I want to do that." He said, "Are you sure?" And I said, "Yes." So I put my daughter in a Moses basket at my feet, rested my foot on her belly because that calmed her, and wrote a pilot script called "War Correspondents," about four female journalists who drink a lot and have a lot of fun while they cover a war. I loved it, but then we went to war, and ABC felt the subject was unseemly under the circumstances. They asked if I'd be interested in writing something else. So I sat back down at my computer and thought about it. If they didn't want to make a show about war correspondents, then I had to figure out what they did want to make a show about. I asked, "What are they interested in?" And my agent said, "Bob Iger wants to have a medical show." I came up with *Grey's Anatomy*. It got picked up, and we shot the pilot in very quick succession.

Grey's was basically me writing about my friends and me—only the characters happen to be surgeons. It felt like I'd put pages of my diary into a script for television, and I was startled that people responded. It felt a little like standing naked in front of everyone, which took some getting used to. What kept the scripts honest was that I stuck to what I knew and what I knew about the people around me. I tried to be truthful about their emotions. The specifics are different because the show involves doctors and fictional characters, but there is something of me and my friends and family on every page. There's a lot in there that's really personal to me, and it never occurred to me that anybody would find that stream of consciousness interesting in the way that they did.

Part of what was interesting when we were casting *Grey's* was that everyone made such a fuss over the fact that it's multicultural. That was strange to me. I wanted the show to look like the world I live in, and I live in a multicultural world. We all live in a multicultural world. Maybe we don't spend as much time with people of other cultures as we should, but there is no denying the world is multicultural. I'm a post–Civil Rights Movement baby, and I wanted *Grey's* to look like a post–Civil Rights Movement world.

It wasn't like I wanted the show to include this many characters of color and that many white characters. It was more about the fact that Hollywood is broken: In every script I read, if a character's race isn't defined, it's assumed to be white. That's always creeped me out, the idea that unless specified otherwise, the world is white. That doesn't make any sense to me. So when we cast the show, we said that we would bring in people of every color for every role and that we wouldn't worry about anything other than finding the best actor for the part. And that's what we did.

My next show, *Private Practice*, started as an experiment. The network wanted another show, and I thought, well, let's see if we can do it. Five years later we're still going strong, which is amazing to me. It has been fun and an education as well, in terms of juggling more than one show.

I tell young writers that you need to be willing to make coffee—great coffee. Try to get your foot in the door. If you can get a job at even the lowest level, as the lowest assistant in the industry, take it. Then do the job better than anyone who has ever done it before. I've seen too many people who say they want to be in the business but don't want to do the work to get there. If you're willing to pay the dues to get where you need to go, you'll get noticed. Eventually someone like me will say, "That girl gets amazing coffee. I wonder why she works so hard." She'll get promoted, she'll be asked if she has ever written anything, her script will be read. That's how you get somewhere in this town.

Beyond making good coffee, if you really want to be a writer, you need to be writing every day. You have to be honest with yourself: If you're not writing things, you're not a writer. It's the only job in this business that you can create out of thin air. If you write really well, if you have a great script, it doesn't matter who you are or what you've done, someone is going to want to buy it, because there's money to be made from it. It's about producing the pages. I wrote my way out of my little administrative assistant position. That's how you do it. The self-discipline part ranks pretty high. If I hadn't been writing every day, my life would never have changed. Writing is a muscle that needs to be exercised. I truly believe that. That's why I can write scripts as quickly as I can. I've been exercising that muscle for a long time.

The state of African American women TV writers is abysmal. The numbers are low. Though there are diversity programs that help to get more writers of color in the door, I'm not sure they're the answer. I've thought about it a lot, to the point of being obsessed. I've mentored and brought along women writers I would like to see get their own shows one day, but it's more about figuring out why in the world access is simply easier for white writers. What's going on with that? Where's the disconnect? Why aren't those other voices as valued? Why aren't they sought out? I don't know the answers. People often ask if it was harder for me, being a woman of color, and I don't know if it was or wasn't. It's not like I can know how it would have been if I wasn't black. In any case, there's something wrong here and we have to figure out what it is.

The most gratifying part of my work is when people write letters or find me on Twitter or walk up to me in the grocery store and tell me that something I did changed their life. One woman came up to me and said, "I watched an episode of your show and went upstairs and told my husband that I want a divorce." She said, "I realized that we didn't have any magic." Another woman came up to me and said, "I diagnosed myself with breast cancer because of something I saw on your show." These things are amazing. We did a rape episode of *Private Practice*, in which one of our main characters is brutally assaulted. At the end of the episode, we put out a PSA telling people to go to the Rape, Abuse, and Incest National Network, and we crashed their Web site with the number of people seeking help. These are the moments when I feel most gratified.

The biggest influences in my life have been the strong women in my own family. I would also add Toni Morrison to that list. I wanted to be Toni Morrison when I was growing up, and I wrote long pages of really bad prose trying to be her. I finally met her a couple of years ago. We had dinner together, and it was an extraordinary experience because she is a woman and a writer and she's strong and she's brilliant and she's amazing and she's human. It was delightful to get to see all that. She has a Nobel Prize. Her magic and creativity continue to influence me.

I'm inspired by a lot of things. I'm inspired by television programs that I watch. I'm inspired by my family, my friends, certain songs, and pieces of art. I'm inspired by anything that feels like it speaks to the human condition. I can find inspiration almost anywhere. Without question, I'm most proud of my child. I'm passionate about trying to make this world better for her. I'm passionate about my job and what I do. I'm lucky to be able to do the thing I love for a living. The minute it stops being interesting and exciting is the moment I will stop doing it. I want to be inspired every day. I want to come to work excited to walk into my office and excited to be walking onto a soundstage. I'm not doing what I do for the money, I'm doing it because I love it. Now I have two shows that I've written on the air at the same time. I just want to keep pushing the envelope, to keep myself creatively stimulated, and to keep going in this business I love.

Shaun Robinson

Shaun Robinson is an Emmy Award–winning journalist who rose to prominence as an anchor and correspondent for Access Hollywood. *She is the author of* Exactly as I Am, *a book for teen girls on building self-esteem. She is also the 2011 recipient of the prestigious Dove Real Beauty Award. A Detroit native, she is a graduate of Spelman College in Atlanta.*

✳

Faith is the most powerful of all forces!" That has been the driving theme throughout my entire life—faith in God and faith in the abilities He gave me. I grew up in Detroit in an average lower-middle-class family. Both my parents worked for the city. My mom was of the Baha'i faith, and my dad was Protestant. However, my grandma was Catholic, so I ended up attending Catholic school, because she convinced my parents I would get a much better education there. I'll never forget taking my first Communion. I was six years old, and all us girls were sporting our little frilly white dresses and walking up to the alter holding our hands in prayer position. I remember there being candles everywhere, and the smell of scented smoke. On the wall before us was a gigantic painting of a black man with a beard and a white robe. I didn't really understand *who* He was, but I knew I was supposed to ask Him for stuff and say "thank you" when I got it.

I remember always saying my prayers at night on my knees against my little bed. There was a long list of people in my family whom I wanted God to bless. My family is very large and interesting in that, through marriages, divorces, and remarriages, there are many stepparents and half siblings and folks we call "cousin" but who aren't actually blood relatives. I have a total of six half siblings and stepsiblings, but we just call each other brothers and sisters. I think what made my family unique was that everybody always got along very well. My mom and stepmom were very friendly, as were my dad and stepdad. My dad and mom, who divorced when I was a little girl, live down the street from each other and still go to breakfast together at least once a week. My grandmother helped care for my stepgrandmother (who was married to my grand-mother's ex-husband) when she was dying of cancer. I've just never experienced that clash of exes who don't get along. I wish every family had that kind of love.

The importance of family has always been emphasized, and that bond has been a true blessing throughout my life. My cousin Donald, who used to love running down our family tree, would always tell me, "Baby, no matter how big you get, never forget where you came from." And I never have. While my hometown has suffered from a tough reputation, I am always proud to say I'm from Detroit. The city is made up of many hard-working, wonderful people who take great pride in their neighborhoods and communities. It's my city and I love it. My people are there, and they will never leave.

One of my early inspirations to get into journalism was a Detroit television anchor named Beverly Payne. And afternoon TV gave me Stymie and Buckwheat on *The Little Rascals*. That was about it. The evening news would come on, and there sat Ms. Payne. Regal, poised, beautiful, and smart. And she had skin like mine. I would sit and watch her, mesmerized. I remember thinking, "I want to be like her when I grow up."

I went to a pretty famous high school, Cass Technical, which was known for its tough curriculum. It was a public school, but you had to have high enough grades to get in. I focused on the performing arts while I was there. I loved the stage and still have the *Dracula* program from tenth grade; I played the role of Wilhelmina, which my mother raves about to this day.

After I graduated from high school, I moved to Atlanta to attend Spelman Col-lege. It was the first time I had ever been away from home—I was a little scared but very excited at the same time. I chose Spelman because of its excellent reputation for the liberal arts and because I had many relatives in Georgia, which made it feel a lit-tle like home. (My grandmother's father, Ben, was from Georgia. He had twenty-two children—eleven by his first wife, and eleven by his second wife, and *both* wives were named Lizzie. So I had folks all over Georgia.)

When young women who are considering college ask me about my experience at Spelman, I tell them it's like a sisterhood. After you graduate, if you cross paths with another woman who went to Spelman, even if she didn't go at the same time you did, you greet each other with "Hello, my Spelman sister!" There is an instant camaraderie among women who went to school there. An important factor in my choice to attend Spelman was that students are taught to dedicate their lives to serving others, which was something my mom and dad had already instilled in me. My parents, including my stepdad and stepmom, always taught me that "to whom much is given, much is required."

I majored in English and minored in mass communications. When I was a junior, one of my journalism teachers chose me to host a local Atlanta cable show called *Open Studio*. It was a very small show that featured guests from the community talking about the issues of the day. It was one of my first times reading a teleprompter, and I'm sure I wasn't very good at it. I don't even want to look back at those tapes. But I truly loved it. I felt (mostly) at ease in front of the camera and enjoyed talking to the guests to find out what they were passionate about.

The summer after my junior year, I went back home to Detroit and got a reporting internship at a very small local television station. I wasn't making any money, but I was learning how to write, edit, and produce a story, which was exactly the foundation I needed to begin building my career in broadcasting. After I graduated from college, I went back to that station and asked them for a paying job. Because I had worked hard and they liked my work the previous summer, the news director hired me, but they only had the budget to hire me part-time. So I took the job, and I also signed up with a temp agency that got me a position doing office work to supplement my income. Because I was such a hard worker, the TV station finally hired me full-time as an anchor and reporter. Soon after, I created a talk show at the station that became extremely popular. I talked to the mayor and celebrities, discussed homosexuality in the black community, and did fashion and cooking segments. The show was one of the first of its kind in the city, and the local newspaper wrote an article about me, calling me "Detroit's own Oprah."

I left the station after a few years because I felt I needed to grow. I never want to get complacent. I briefly moved to Flint, Michigan, where I worked at the local CBS affiliate as an anchor and reporter. I was there for only a few months—my news director kept telling me that he didn't think I was good enough on the air and that I should start looking for another job. At first I was scared; I didn't know how fast I could find something. I quickly started sending out résumé tapes, and in just a couple of weeks I landed a job as a medical reporter at the ABC affiliate in Milwaukee. While there, I won an Associated Press award and an American Cancer Society award for my reporting and also started hosting a talk show called *Milwaukee's Talking,* for which I earned rave reviews.

Though my career was blossoming in Milwaukee, my personal life took another turn. I got married and reluctantly gave up my job to relocate to the city where my husband lived, but the marriage lasted only a year. After it ended, I found myself back at my parents' house in Detroit, in my old bedroom, with no job, feeling like a real failure. The emotional toll was huge. On top of that, my stepfather, whom I was very close to, passed away after a long illness. One of my closest friends, who had been the maid of honor at my wedding, had recently died of lupus. With the deaths of two people very close to me, the end of my marriage, and the huge stumbling block in my career, it was an absolutely horrible time.

My mother kept telling me to get centered and to pray for guidance. Mom was then, and continues to be, my rock. She was dealing with the loss of her husband of almost two decades, and so we needed to be there for each other. My mother has always been a very positive person. If she gets down, she tries to find ways to pick herself back up, like listening to motivational tapes or watching something funny on TV. What I have learned from her is that the pity party cannot last for long. Allow yourself to grieve, but don't wallow in it.

While Mom is the spiritual one, Dad is more the philosophical one. He's the one who keeps me motivated by telling me, "Baby, a setback is a setup for a *comeback*!" He always says not to look at problems emotionally. Rather, try to think of a practical solution to any issue you're dealing with. Think rationally about what you need to do to get back on track, and stay focused.

It was a real struggle to get back in the game. I would send my old résumé tapes out to TV stations, and I would always get asked by news directors why I wasn't working. Saying you left your job to get married gets you a blank stare. I found myself having to beg agents to look at my tape and to represent me. But finally persistence paid off. I landed a job as an anchor-reporter in Austin, Texas. The position allowed me to be back on the air and to cover some really interesting stories. I was able to visit the notorious Huntsville prison and talk to death-row inmates.

I worked really hard, and after only a year I got a job as an anchor-reporter in Miami. This particular station was a pioneer in "breaking news" and flashy graphics. Routinely, I would have to ad-lib over video of news events for hours. The experience was great because it really helped me strengthen my live skills. One of the toughest stories I did involved going to Oklahoma City on the first anniversary of the bombing of the Alfred P. Murrah Federal Building, which killed 168 people and injured close to 700. I will always remember standing in the bedroom of two young brothers who were killed in the daycare center. For the past year, their grandmother had left the room exactly the way it was on the day of the blast.

Eventually, I grew tired of hard news. I no longer had an interest in covering fires, car crashes, hurricanes, and murders. I wanted to do something different. I had always had a desire to do more entertainment stories—I wanted to show more personality and have some fun. So I sent out more tapes and connected with headhunting agencies, and finally *Access Hollywood* called, and I went out to Los Angeles for an interview. I remember sitting on the set of the show, which I had watched on television for years. I was so nervous that I froze during my reading of the teleprompter. I was sure I hadn't done well during my interview, but then a week later my agent called and told me I got the job. I remember thinking, "Wow! My life is about to change!"

One of the most life-changing experiences I had at *Access Hollywood* was being invited by Oprah Winfrey to cover the opening of her Leadership Academy for Girls in Johannesburg, South Africa. It was truly amazing to see these dynamic young black girls—many of whom came from living in shacks in the poorest shantytowns with no running water or electricity—excel in math, reading, and science. They were extraordinarily smart, gifted, and charismatic. It was so emotional for me. I listened to stories about having to do homework by candlelight, sharing one outdoor toilet with dozens of other families, or worse: walking to their old schools afraid of being raped. But they valued their education so much that they overcame the obstacles in their way. The girls made me realize how much we complain about things that are truly insignificant.

I won my first Emmy while at *Access Hollywood.* Being able to add that to my list of accomplishments was incredible. But the most thrilling part of my work is that I am seen as a role model by so many young women. I'm very thankful to have a platform that allows me to touch the lives of others.

My mother tells me the only reason God gives you a voice is so you can give back and help other people. That's why I wrote my book, *Exactly as I Am.* I want girls to know that no matter how much money you have, no matter how beautiful or famous you are, we're all the same inside. All of us have doubts. All of us feel we don't measure up in some way. When you get right down to it, it's not any of those things that make you feel good about yourself—it's knowing that you are loved and that, as Oprah says, you have a right to be here "because you were born." As long as I touch the lives of young people and give them some hope and inspiration to achieve their goals and feel good about themselves, I feel I'm doing my job.

More than ever, I know today's girls face challenges that I never did growing up. We all look back on our lives and say, "Wow, I should have done that differently," so I am okay sharing my mistakes with young women so they know, as my dad said, that this life is going to have peaks and valleys, but if you keep the faith, you'll come out on top.

As someone in the public eye, I definitely feel a sense of responsibility for how I conduct myself publicly. I've learned that whether you like it or not, you are under a microscope and people are watching you to see how you act and *react* to circumstances. There are times when I may feel like I didn't conduct myself in the manner in which my mama raised me, so when I pray, I pray that God will make those times glaring to me and lead me to correct them.

Among the keys to happiness, especially in my business, are a sense of humor and the ability to laugh at yourself and your mistakes. Many people in Hollywood feel

they must put forth an image of perfection, and when they don't live up to that, they fall really hard. If you screw up, own up to it, and you'll be surprised by the number of people who will admire you even more. I had an incident with Al Pacino during an interview. I was a little nervous about meeting him because, well, it's Al Pacino. The cameras were rolling, and we were about the start the interview, when I noticed a crumb of food near his mouth. I gave him a signal to wipe it off, and when he didn't respond, I tried to get his publicist's attention to see if she noticed, but she didn't. Finally, I leaned toward him and said, "Mr. Pacino, there's something on your face." I reached within an inch of his mouth to wipe it off and realized the "crumb" was actually a mole. I was mortified. I said, "Oh, I'm so sorry, Mr. Pacino. It's a mole," and everyone, including Al, burst out laughing. He held his head in his hands and said, "Just call me Mole Man!" It turned out to be one of my favorite interviews.

As African American women in our society, we often are not validated—our beauty, our worth, and our value are not acknowledged, and we often feel invisible. When I think back on my life, I will never forget that I come from a family of very strong African American women. Neither one of my grandmothers—Elsie and Sarah—had much at all, but what they did have was love for all their children. When I think back on them working and raising families with very few resources, they seem like superwomen. They made our lives abundantly full. My mother is a true inspiration because she loves me unconditionally and is always there when I need her. She's still my role model, mostly because she has such a kind spirit. In another life, she would have been Mother Teresa. She inspires me every day to be my best and to never forget my strong family roots. She's always there to tell me I can do anything I put my mind to. My mother and father say that, as parents, you want to know that your kids are going to be okay, that they're going to be strong enough to carry on without you. I tell them, "You're never going to have to worry about me. I'm going to be fine. I have a fighting spirit, and you've instilled in me the right values, and you gave me the foundation of prayer, which will take me through the toughest times."

Eventually, I want to have my own show. My strength is the passionate, in-depth interview, and I want to talk to all kinds of people who are changing the world. I want to inspire even more people and motivate them to achieve their goals. When a young woman comes up to me and says, "I want you to know I was inspired because of you," I feel I am doing what I was put on this earth to do.

And when I think about that young girl taking her first Communion and looking up at that wall and seeing that man in the robe with his arms outstretched, I remember what Grandma always told me to say: "Thank you, Lord."

Betye Saar

Betye Saar is an artist known for her collage and assemblage work, her most famous piece being The Liberation of Aunt Jemima. *She is the mother of three daughters and has explored in her art everything from stereotypical African American images to folk traditions, family memorabilia, and the relationship between technology and spirituality.*

✶

I'm a child of the Depression. So, right away, I've got a certain mind-set, a certain attitude about life and work because we didn't have everything we wanted. Some of my strongest childhood memories have to do with sadness. My mother was born in the small town of Perry, Iowa, to an African American–Native American father and an Irish mother. My grandfather's family was from Missouri, from a town on the Mason-Dixon Line, where interracial marriages were not permitted. He and my grandmother went to Perry, where my mother was born. When my mother was nine years old, her mother died. Her father was distraught and unable to care for her, so he sent her back to Missouri to live with his family, with whom she grew up.

My mother always had a trace of sadness about her. I think sadness is in one's DNA, or at least that's the way it feels to me. I believe emotions are passed down, like physical characteristics. I mention this because it has to do with the way I express myself through my art. Many of my pieces deal with memory and sadness, which relates to my mother, who not only lost her mother when she was a child but also was estranged from her father for some time afterward. Then she fell in love with my father, who was a wonderful man. They got married and had a nice home, but he passed away at age thirty-one, leaving her to care for three young children alone.

I'm from a family that likes to do things with their hands. My mother's mother hand-painted china. My sister and I grew up project oriented. We were always sewing and making clothes for ourselves. For special holidays, like Christmas, my mother would make us dolls, and we would make clothes for them. We made Easter baskets for each other or May Day baskets, which we filled with flowers. We made valentines. We made drawings or paintings for each other; art was always a part of our lives. Our house was always decorated in a beautiful way. My mother loved beauty and wanted to have a nice home. (We all like to collect stuff and make it part of our environment.)

Growing up, I was interested in art school, but art schools were segregated. When I was young, I knew only one person of color, a GI, who had the opportunity to go to art school. But there were organizations that were supportive of bright young people who needed financial help, and so my sister and I both got scholarships to UCLA. I studied design because becoming a fine artist, someone who made paintings, seemed to be too far-fetched a goal. We didn't even know any fine artists. Our family had only just emerged from the Depression, and I had to be practical. I knew I could support myself through interior decorating.

My sister and I graduated from UCLA in 1949 and got jobs as social workers in Pasadena. I lived at home until I was transferred to work in Los Angeles, where I began to make a life of my own. I was about twenty-two and still uncertain, but then I began meeting people who were interested in jazz and art. I met a woman who was a sculptor, and she threw great parties where I was introduced to other artists. That's when I began to find my people. Not "my people" racially but people who shared my interest in the arts, whether dance or drama or visual arts or writing or whatever. Through them I found the creative element in my community and in Los Angeles. Other friends came to L.A., and we formed an African American cultural scene, mostly centered on the visual arts. It was the early sixties, just the beginning of the black American art movement in Los Angeles; I was just becoming aware of art as something to exhibit and of the larger African American art community.

As more and more African Americans became involved in the arts—in drawing and painting, printmaking, and sculpture—we created our own spaces to make and show our work. These were often in community centers or churches, because there was still segregation and we were, for the most part, invisible to the white art world. Every once in a while, if there was an open call for work, or a competition, you could submit something and get in because the judges didn't know your color. But we generally didn't have access to the professional galleries that were open at the time. They were filled with white guys who'd come in and gone to art school through the GI Bill. The scene was masculine; women, let alone black women, just didn't have much opportunity to show in those galleries.

My first exhibit in a professional gallery was at the Palos Verdes Art Center, and it opened two weeks after I'd had my third child. I'd gone back to school to get a teaching credential and taken a print-making class, which was a turning point: I went from being someone who did projects, someone who made stuff with her hands or designed things, to being a fine artist, someone who pursues painting, sculpture, and printmaking. This shift marked the beginning of my journey—my real journey—into being a professional artist. I was the only person of color to participate in the Art Center show, and that, too, was a crossroads.

Even though I was making art, it was a long time before I had a career as an artist, because I was still trying to find my voice through the medium. I began with printmaking, turned to drawing, and then I shifted to making work about my life. One day I went to an exhibition in Pasadena and saw Joseph Cornell's boxes. All of a sudden, I realized, "Oh, it's just putting stuff in boxes, and it tells a story. It's like writing a book with objects, your paintings and your drawings." So I began to make objects. My children would go with me to flea markets, to yard sales, to antique shops; we were always collecting stuff. That's how they became artists, too, by collecting stuff and making it into art. Eventually, I began to show this new work, which was another crossroads because it was sculpture—not drawings or prints.

I finally told myself that I was really an artist in 1974, when I received a grant from the National Endowment for the Arts. I remember looking at the check and thinking, "Somebody thinks I'm a real artist." It seems trite to say that money defined my start, but it was money from a government source, and it meant, "We're rewarding you for being an artist." In my head something clicked; a voice inside said, "I'm a real artist. I'm a real artist." I'd always had a creative lifestyle, but that check, that monetary reward, gave me an inner confidence that this is what I can do: I can have a creative *life*. I didn't go looking for the career; my career found me. I just wanted to make these things, and then I would put them out there. It just felt comfortable, like I'd put on a nice, cozy coat or sweater and realized, "It fits! This fits me. This is what I can do. This is what I can be."

I often feel I'm outside of what's popular in the art world. I never had the stroke for what's mainstream, because it goes against my flow. My flow takes me to different places, wandering along paths on a meandering journey. I consider myself a narrative artist because I tell stories with my materials. I work in what's called mixed media: I find things, and those particular things generate ideas. Like, I was in Maine, and I found this little birdcage, and it led to a series about cages, about the cage as a metaphor for one's life—or personality or social issues or political issues or whatever. When I was younger, I was inspired by nature and my family. My children were quite young, and I would draw them or make prints about them. Now I'm more inspired by materials, by ordinary objects, or by thoughts, and I use those materials and ideas to make different series—for instance, collages about racial issues within the black community, about the names we call each other, and about what we consider to be good and not so good. Or I'll do a series based on washboards or trays. These were the exhibitions "Colored" and "Cages," and my iconic piece *The Liberation of Aunt Jemima*. My path is about finding something, maybe an object, and then taking off with it.

To be an artist is special because art connects people in a certain way—just like music or drama connects people. But art is especially meaningful because *how* you look at it and connect with it is very private. I feel fortunate in that I continue to be inspired and that I still have the opportunity to use my creativity, to share myself and my message, and to leave an imprint on our culture—an imprint that touches people and perhaps makes them want to explore or know more about art or about an aspect of themselves.

If I wasn't an artist, I'd be a writer. I already write in a way, but my materials are my language: I don't use words, I use colors. I don't use paragraphs, I use objects. And when I'm making something, I'm not thinking about the materials. I'm thinking about the story. I'm on automatic-artist pilot, and it just comes together. I feel fortunate that I can do that. I'm not always working with my hands, but I'm always working. I'm always thinking about whatever it is or getting inspired about it.

I love being an artist, but I consider being a mom my greatest achievement. I've raised three daughters, all of whom have found ways to express themselves and discover what makes them whole. To me, my family always comes first. My family is my first priority.

Nina Shaw

Nina Shaw is a graduate of Barnard College and Columbia Law School. She is a founding partner of the law firm Del, Shaw, Moonves, Tanaka, Finkelstein & Lezcano, which opened in Los Angeles in 1989, and caters to many high-profile African American clients, along with many others throughout the entertainment industry.

*

I've always been very focused, even as a young child. I started school before programs like Head Start, and before kindergarten was mandatory. When I began first grade I was totally unprepared; I didn't know the alphabet or my colors—I didn't have any readiness skills, but I caught on quickly. I remember our reading period: The teacher would go one by one around the classroom, and everyone had to read a page from our reader, the Dick and Jane reader. I sat at my little desk, counting all the students ahead of me and trying to figure out the page I would read if everyone was present—along with the page I would read if someone happened to be absent. Then I went home and practiced all the pages in between in front of the bathroom mirror until I read them perfectly. I remember being so anxious about doing a good job. And this was only *Fun with Dick and Jane*!

I grew up in Harlem and attended public school there until sixth grade, when I was bused to a public school in Astoria, Queens. I attended junior high and high school in the Bronx. I graduated from William Howard Taft High School, which was a very rough-and-tough school in a very rough-and-tough neighborhood. At Taft and in that neighborhood you quickly learned to read people and situations, and I learned that how one responded was critical. If you said the wrong thing, messed with the wrong person, ignored the wrong person, even walked on the wrong side of the street—there were so many ways that one could get into trouble. Consequently, I became really good at assessing and judging situations and how to react to them.

The great part was that even at Taft, there were groups of students and teachers who were focused on learning. I was in the honors program, and was fortunate in having many great classes and wonderful teachers. When I went to college, I wasn't as prepared as some of my classmates, but I was confident of my intellect and caught up quickly. I went to Barnard College, in part because my high school English teacher had gone there. She encouraged me to apply and was an invaluable resource because the high school guidance department was overwhelmed and understaffed, and it was difficult for them to pay attention to what students wanted to do beyond high school.

My mother had some college, but she put a very high premium on being knowledgeable and well-read, more so than on being traditionally educated. Every morning she sent me to buy her the *New York Times* and the *Daily News*, and then every afternoon, the *Journal American* and another afternoon newspaper. In our house, we were always reading four newspapers a day, and I recall reading about the Cuban Missile Crisis and having a keen sense of what was going on in the world. I also went to the library almost every day. I loved history and devoured John Hope Franklin's *From Slavery to Freedom: A History of African Americans* and *The Story of Civilization*, by Will and Ariel Durant. Because there were five of us kids, my mom wouldn't let us stay in the house on rainy days and drive her crazy. Instead, she'd pack a lunch and put us on the Amsterdam Avenue bus. We would then transfer to a crosstown bus and spend the day at the Metropolitan Museum of Art or the Museum of Natural History. I don't think she thought anything of putting her eight- and nine-year-olds on a bus and saying, "Go spend the day at the museum—it doesn't matter which one."

Self-reliance was emphasized when I grew up—with five kids, everyone had to pitch in. There was a schedule, and we all had chores. We were expected to take care of ourselves as well as look out for one another. As one of the older children, I had to help care for my younger brothers and sister. My stepfather was a cop. He worked a regular shift during the day, and like many cops of that era, he drove a cab in his off hours. My mom worked the night shift at the post office. Typically, she would start dinner before she left the house, and then my older sister and I would finish up, get the other kids fed, and make sure they did their homework. Then we set aside plates for my mom and stepfather so they could have dinner when they got home, cleaned the kitchen, and did our homework.

My maternal great-grandmother was an enormous influence on me. She grew up in Charlottesville, Virginia, at a time when there was no high school for colored children. After the Civil War, her parents and grandparents had taken advantage of the educational opportunities provided by the Freedmen's Bureau, a federal agency that aided freed slaves. So, by comparison, my great-grandmother had fewer educational opportunities than the generation before her. Her mother-in-law graduated from "normal school," which was a school set up by the Freedmen's Bureau to provide newly freed people with high school and college edu-

cations so they could teach and "raise up the race." The curriculum was rigorous and included Greek, Latin, astronomy, and physics. When Reconstruction ended, however, and Jim Crow laws were enacted, the normal schools were phased out. So in Charlottesville, if you wanted to educate your children beyond eighth grade, they had to go to what are now many of the historically black colleges. My great-grandmother left Charlottesville to attend Oberlin College in Ohio in 1910. While Oberlin was not a historically black college, it was among the first colleges in the United States to admit colored people. She couldn't afford to finish, but she was an enormously well-read woman.

She passed down her love of reading to her daughter, my grandmother, and to my mother and to me.

In my high school yearbook, my entry reads "Future Lawyer." At the time, I didn't have a keen sense of what lawyers did other than what I'd seen on television, but I was interested in history and what constitutes a civil society. When you read a lot of history, you can't help but consider the law and what it means for advancing civil rights. I grew up during the Civil Rights Movement, and famous lawyers like Thurgood Marshall were superheroes to me. I did well in law school and was offered a number of jobs. After finishing school, I moved to Los Angeles and joined a top-notch firm, O'Melveny & Myers. At O'Melveny, I was fortunate to work in the entertainment law department. One of O'Melveny's more prominent clients was the television producer Norman Lear, who was responsible for iconic television series such as: *All in the Family*, *The Jeffersons*, and *One Day at a Time.* As a young associate I worked on projects that were precedent-setting, and in some cases groundbreaking in the way television deals were structured. I couldn't have asked for a better introduction to entertainment law.

The entertainment industry is very closed, and in large part, one is hired as a result of connections, which I didn't have. Law firms in that era had few African Americans or women. You could count women and African American partners on one hand and have fingers left. Ultimately I realized that if I was going to get anywhere in the business, I would have to start my own firm. One of the reasons there are a lot of successful minority and female businesspeople in the entertainment industry is that if you can meet the talent, and sell yourself successfully to talent, you get hired. I've always been obsessively—and compulsively—concerned about doing a good job, which for me means, in part, being as well prepared as is humanly possible. I feel confident about my abilities. I never walk into a room and think, "Oh my God, everyone here knows more than I do." I'm more apt to think, "You wouldn't necessarily be in this room if you had to take my path." I am always confident, and I think that when you're confident and can deliver, others believe in you and you rise to the task.

I recently met with a young woman who was already defeated, and I was just amazed. I reminded her of a number of good things about her—and there were quite a few — including that she had gone to a top law school. Perhaps she hadn't done as well as she could have, but by getting into that school and graduating from it, she was ahead of a bunch of other people. Just the same, she kept beating herself up. I said to her, "Next time you walk into a room for a meeting, you walk up to them and you extend your hand to them. Then you explain why you're special and why you're deserving of the opportunity they have to offer. Don't you ever walk into a room again and be apologetic. If people ask you questions about your background, answer them as forthrightly as possible." Ultimately people feel about us how we feel about ourselves. I'm proud of the fact that I've been able to have an enormous impact on the young people entering the entertainment industry. I've mentored many of them and tried to make opportunities for them. I think of all the people I've helped as my legacy in the entertainment industry.

I talk to people all the time who tell me they want to get into entertainment law, but then I find out they don't go to the movies and they don't watch TV. I mean, why would you want to do this if you don't seem to have any interest in entertainment? It's just like any other career: you have to love it to succeed at it. Success in this industry doesn't happen because you think it's something you *might* like to do. I tell young people, "Do your homework. You have to be knowledgeable about the entertainment business, about the people in the business, and about the history of the business." My advice is to get as much exposure to the arts as you possibly can, because that's the substance of it. Do your research and then be tenacious. No one starts a business and no one succeeds at anything, unless they are passionate about it.

I had a wonderfully supportive family. My mom is my biggest inspiration because she fostered my inquisitive nature and always demanded the best of me. When I was growing up, she would ask me, "Why would you do that? How could you do it differently?" Unlike a lot of people of her generation, she encouraged me to find my own way. She's not a churchgoer at all, but she's the most moral person I know. She truly lives by the golden rule. I remember once when I was a teenager and we were walking down the street, I made a derogatory comment about someone who passed us, about either the way she was dressed or the way she looked. My mother stopped me and said,

"Nina, do you want to be the kind of person that people can't trust, who people think you are saying something mean about them as soon as they walk away?" Her clear sense of right and wrong formed the kind of person I've become. She's a thinker and likes to talk things through. She'd say, "Let's figure this out," or "What do you think?" and we would have a long conversation about whatever it was. I realize now that not all girls were so lucky.

I'm passionate about issues that relate to girls, the education of girls, and the reproductive rights of girls and women. When I was twelve or thirteen years old, I woke up in the middle of the night because I heard an ambulance. My mom explained to me that the ambulance was there because the woman next door had tried to perform an abortion on herself. We talked about how alone this woman must have felt and how desperate she must have been about having a child she couldn't take care of. I remember being so struck by the sadness of the situation. The thought of this woman—home alone in such utter desperation, trying to perform an abortion because she felt she had to—is seared into my memory. When I was a teenager, abortions were still illegal, and so self-abortions weren't an uncommon occurrence. As women, we should be able to control our destinies when it comes to family planning. Everyone has the right to be a parent, but frankly not everyone is ready to be a parent, and the children ultimately suffer. This realization eventually led to my decision to join the board of Planned Parenthood and to become a big sister in the Big Brothers Big Sisters organization.

I've come to accept that you can't always balance it all—work, parenting, being a wife. There are going to be days when you screw something up, and then you have to take the long view. It's not any one individual day that matters; it's what you give consistently day in and day out. So yes, there were many times I felt like "Oh, my poor kids!" but they're adults now and they're fine. They're independent and very loving people. There were also times when I'd wake up in the middle of the night thinking, "I didn't get to that deal or I didn't get to that contract or that phone call." Part of getting older is learning to accept that you can't do it all. I try to compartmentalize when I can and start each day fresh, not dwelling on the day before. Frankly, there are enough people out in the world ready to criticize; it is important not to do it to yourself.

I also think it's important to encourage independence. I remember one day someone called me and said they saw one of my kids walking down Sunset Boulevard near the 405 freeway, and I said, "Yeah, you probably did see her because I bet she spent her bus fare and she's walking home." Sure enough, she told me later she'd spent her bus money, so I had this discussion with her about budgeting and choices. She'd made her choice about spending money, and while I don't think walking down Sunset Boulevard was necessarily the wisest choice, she only had to do it once before she figured that saving her money for the bus was a better idea.

Though I'm very proud of the business I've built, at the end of the day, I'm most proud of my family. I'm proud that my husband and I decided to provide the youngest generation of our family with as much access to education and the means to bettering themselves as it has been possible for us to provide. We want each and every one of them to fulfill their potential, to go to college, and to go on to graduate school, and so far we've been pretty successful. We've helped them attend college, and more importantly, we've made it a special priority to focus on those who might not have wanted to continue their education. We've encouraged them to make their education a priority.

I try not to have too many regrets when it comes to life—I don't think it's useful. Are there situations I could and would have handled differently if given the opportunity? Yes, and I hope I've learned from them and will handle similar situations differently in the future. But I don't have something that I wanted to do with my life that I haven't had the chance to do. I don't have those kinds of regrets.

Raven-Symoné

Raven-Symoné was a young child star on The Cosby Show *and went on to star on her own Disney show,* That's So Raven*, and in the* Cheetah Girls *franchise and many other films. In 2011 her show* State of Georgia *ran on ABC Family.*

⭐

My mom came from Louisiana. She wasn't rich or from a trust, so she looked around and said, "I gotta get out of here." She went to college, where she found her man. She stuck by him, worked with him, and had a baby—me. Then she followed her baby's dreams. I don't have any big bruises from my mom—on either my psyche or my body—and I'm proud of her because we've finally reached the point in our relationship where we're friends.

My dad is superamazing. He's the first reason I'm an actress today. The second is Bill Cosby, but it was my daddy who knew how to find the right rooms to go into, the right words to say to get me the auditions that a young African American female would not be likely to get. He went out on a limb to help me live the dream that I had, the dream that *we* had, and he tells me to this day, "You know the only reason it worked? Because we were all involved. We all worked toward a goal. If one person had faltered, then you wouldn't be where you are." We all did it together, but he was the glue.

When I first started working on *The Cosby Show*, I was three years old. The moment I stepped on-set, I realized that I was working. I auditioned in front of Sidney Poitier, who was a close friend of Bill Cosby's. He said, "You need to meet Bill," and then he took me to meet him. Later on I heard that Bill Cosby hadn't wanted anybody else on the show, but he accepted me and taught me pretty much everything I know. It's hard because I don't remember exactly what I learned; it was subconscious learning, which is the best sort because it sticks longer. My parents tell me I loved it, and they don't mess around. They would always say to me, "You wanted to do this. This is a job. This is a check. This is not a game." But they also told me I could leave anytime. So one day, to see if they really meant it, I said, "Okay, I'm leaving." And they were like, "Okay, fine. What are you going to do now?" And I was like, I can't go to college yet

because I'm on a show and too young, and I don't really have anything else to fall back on. I knew that even if I did try something else, I wouldn't be as happy as I was on-set with people that I love and characters I can play. And nothing could compare to seeing how happy people were when they watched the show. So I said to myself, "Why would I quit? That's really stupid." Right now, I don't think I'll ever quit acting.

As I get older, I'm learning about other parts of the industry, which I adore. There's always a lot going on. Sitcoms are my first love. Some people have to do movies. I need to do sitcoms. I love that there's an audience in front of me. I love that it's a play in a sense but with a new script every week. I love that I can sit with a character — cross my fingers — longer than a year. Hopefully, I can mold a character into what I want her to be over the course of time. And putting the actor stuff aside, I love the family that you create on a set. I love the fact that to this day I still talk to Rondell Sheridan, who played my father on *That's So Raven*. I still talk to Kyle Massey, Anneliese van der Pol, Malcolm-Jamal Warner, Mark Curry, and other people from that and other sets because we built relationships by being together every day. You're all there to do a job, but at the same time, you can't help but put that aside and ask, "What do you need? What's up?" You grow with each other and that builds love. I love doing movies, too, don't get me wrong. But in movies, you're only on the set for a few months, and then it's on to the next, which leaves me feeling like, "Aww, you guys." I guess I'm a baby that way.

I don't have heroes in the traditional sense. I have mentors and people I look up to, but I've really stopped putting anyone in particular on a pedestal. The word *hero* has been used for so long and suggests something so unattainable that it scares me. To me, everyone has heroic abilities, characteristics, or talents that we can all look up to. I mean, even a homeless person's a hero for actually standing there, getting people's blank stares every day, and still grinding for his cause. Obama's a hero because of what he has accomplished. My mom's a hero for having two babies and still looking good. My brother's a hero for just being alive, for being a black man and not a statistic. I can find the hero in everyone.

For my last birthday, my mom asked me what I wanted. I told her I didn't want anything, that I have too much stuff already. Instead, I asked Ms. Debbie Allen to hook me up with some tickets to see Andrea Bocelli, my mom's favorite person in the whole world. When I gave her the tickets on my birthday, she was like, "But what do *you* want?" And I'm like, "Do not give me a thing. I'm giving *you* something because you birthed me." I cried because she was so happy and she wasn't expecting it. I just liked that a lot. I think this way of being comes from the fact that I've been so blessed in my life. I really don't want for anything, which I credit to my parents, whether it's a compliment or something else. I mean, you can't really get happiness unless you share your happiness. I'm passionate about making people happy, whether it makes me happy or not. This is the unhealthy part of me and something I'm working on. I'd rather see a smile on somebody else's face than on my own. I'll give and give until I'm sick in bed. It's beautiful to give, but you can't give away all of yourself. Giving's complicated because it can be a good or bad thing.

I know who I am, but I don't believe the hype of "Raven-Symoné." I don't believe in all the stuff that people say, which isn't the truth anyway. Even my friends are like, "You're Raven-Symoné." And I'm like, "I'm only Raven-Symoné when I am on the red carpet." I love it, don't get me wrong, but I want to be clear that it's not all that I am.

I'm not defined by it because I have so much more to me that no one besides friends and family will ever know.

You have to realize that what we have to do to look a certain way on TV is not possible without help. And that's just the truth. I don't wake up looking like the girl on the red carpet. Whether you blog your opinion about me or not, whether you like what I look like or not, I really don't care. But it takes a lot of money and effort and help to look that way. People got so mad at me because I started admitting that I have a weave. I'm like, "My hair is healthy because I wear weaves. Don't get mad." I wear apparatuses to keep the curves tight. Don't get mad because I'm telling secrets. Girls go through a lot, including going under the knife, to look a certain way. Sweetheart, don't do something permanent. It's not worth it because styles will change, and then you're going to be messed up. It's a crazy world out there, and I want to tell the truth about everything. I have to work just as hard as you do to look a certain way.

When young people tell me they want to get into the business, my first question is "Do you want to be famous or do you want a career?" Usually they don't know how to answer because they're young and don't know what the word career means or calls for. If they say they want to be famous, I'm like, "Well, you know what? Go on about your business." But then if they say they want a career, I say, "You know, this is hard work. You can turn on the TV and see all the happy parts about it, but you're going to need to wake up at four o'clock in the morning and be in hair and makeup for three hours. You'll need to go on the set, do a photo shoot, leave, do an interview, leave, get on the plane, go to New York, and do it all over again for at least two months. Can you handle that?" The part of the job that people see on TV is like 5 percent of it. There's so much more that goes on behind the scenes. People have to be ready for that. They need to know that this is a job. This is not popping bottles of champagne and all the kinds of stuff that people think it is. People's lives, livelihoods, and bank accounts are at stake, and you have to take it seriously. There are different ways to go about it, but I can only offer the information I've got. Just remember that anybody can take your place at any time.

I always tell young people to make sure they're ready for it. And if they're ready for it, it's the most awesome job in the world. You get to meet people you see in movies and on TV. Doors are opened that you never dreamed would be. You have access to information and knowledge—good and bad—that you thought you'd never have. People listen to you in a way you never thought they would. And you get to really explore every nook and cranny of every desire. Yes, there's enough room for us all, especially now that reality TV is here, but we also need doctors, teachers, people to clean up the mess that other people have left. There are lots of other awesome jobs in other industries. Go and search. Don't just look at TV and say, "That's what I want to do," because it's hard. Go and search. Find what you're passionate about first and then worry about how to make money at it.

I keep a list in a jade box in my house of everything I want to accomplish before I die. So far, I've only checked off three things, and it's two pages long. I've written out all the details: family, business, and personal because—thank you, Dr. Wayne Dyer—you have to work backward from the end. I already see where I'm going to be, so when a window opens, when options are put in front of me, I can choose the path that will get me there. There are always going to be twists and turns, but I can't lose sight of my goals. Trust me, there have been many things that looked supertempting along the way, things that would have allowed me to retire a long time ago, but they weren't part of my plan. I'm sticking to my plan. I will sit here in my little house until the right path presents itself so I can reach my goal.

I'm twenty-five years old now. Hopefully, when I'm thirty-five, I'll be in the third season of my talk show. By then I hope to be married with two or three kids. My home base will be in Colorado—I've already looked at property; I haven't bought it, but I know where it's going to be. Then, by about forty, I'll have written a book that tells my story—all the parts I haven't told before and all the parts I've yet to go through. It's all planned. After I've done the book, I want to sit at home and paint the sky and call my accountant every three days to say, "How's the bank account doing? Can my kids survive?" I want to be rich in the broader sense, not just wealthy. I know money isn't everything, but in our materialistic world, I want to make sure that my kids are okay. I want them to work for what they have, but I also want them to know that their mom worked hard for them—and not just for herself.

Susan L. Taylor

Susan L. Taylor started at Essence *in 1970 and rose through the ranks to become editor in chief, a position she held from 1981 to 2000, after which she became the editorial director until 2007. Today, she is CEO of the National CARES Mentoring Movement, which she founded as Essence CARES in 2005, just after the devastation of Hurricane Katrina.*

✴

I grew up in Spanish Harlem in a household that was strong, stable, and mostly Victorian in its attitudes. Babs and Lawrence were older parents when my brother Larry, and I were born. Daddy hailed from Saint Kitts, and Mommy was from Trinidad. They met and married in Harlem in the 1930s, but it would be almost a decade before they had children. Mommy was in her late thirties, and Daddy was nearly fifty when I was born. Lawrence was a good man. He was smart, confident, and oh so stern. He didn't smoke or drink, and I never once heard him swear. He was respectful and, like the men of his day, always tipped his hat when greeting a woman. He supported his family and came home to our small tenement apartment each night after closing his women's clothing store. We never wondered where Daddy was; we always knew. His world was certain—he was either running his business or at home in his chair. But emotionally he seemed miles away. Daddy was silent, sullen. I have no memory of his laughter or of him hugging anyone—not even my mother. I was a chatty lovebug trapped in a family of quiet people who never seemed to touch. I took my father's gloominess and my mother's sadness and constant criticism personally. I thought they didn't like me.

My grandmother couldn't have been more different. Rhoda Weekes was a lover of life. We called her Mother. She had a big personality, a big heart, a big Buick

Roadmaster, and a big house with a beautiful flower garden and yard in New Jersey. There, Larry and I had bicycles we'd ride throughout the neighborhood, and rooms of our own—unlike in Harlem, where we grew up sleeping in bunk beds in the living room. Englewood, New Jersey, was safe and welcoming. Each summer Mother took us on long stay-over visits to her friend Lynn's home in Brooklyn, to upstate lakes, the white sandy beaches along the Long Island shore, and to the Shinnecock Reservation in South Hampton, where she'd rent a cottage for the family. In contrast to the chaotic lives of the children I was growing up with in Harlem, I had a wonderful childhood, primarily because of my and my parents' values and expectations and my grandmother's generosity and love. When I look back on it, my heart fills with gratitude.

My father's store, Larry's Specialty Shop, was downstairs from our apartment. Daddy was the first black person to own a store in East Harlem. All the businesses in our thriving community, where Harlem folks came to shop, were owned by Eastern European Jews who had fled Hitler's army. I grew up in Daddy's store in the 1950s, learning how to count, make change, and keep the merchandise neat, until finally I graduated to selling stockings, panties, and bras, then blouses and skirts. Entrepreneurship was in our blood. My hardworking West Indian parents never said, "Go to college." It was always, "Start your own business and buy a home." And I did. I started my own business, a cosmetics company, at twenty-four, and I bought a brownstone in Harlem twelve years later.

I didn't go to college until after I had become the editor in chief of *Essence* magazine and increasingly was feeling that I needed to know more about the history of our people, how we had built empires and survived enslavement and such unspeakable acts of violence and were now losing ground. During the twenty-seven years I led the magazine, and to this day, my primary interests have been how to help heal the psyche and soul of black people and move toward unity and productivity. When I joined *Essence* as its beauty editor, I was equipped with only a commercial diploma from John Adams High School in Queens and a cosmetology license, while the editors and art directors I worked with were college graduates, some with advanced degrees and most wickedly smart. Deep down inside, I must have known that the money, celebration, and power that came with my leadership position at *Essence* were sufficient in themselves to make a life that was full and meaningful. But I needed more nourishment, intellectual and spiritual, though at the time no one in my life believed I needed to go to college. I was at the top of my game, leading several Essence Communications ventures. I was well paid and was becoming well known, but a deeper hunger kept gnawing at me. So I enrolled at Fordham University, just across the street from where my beloved daughter, Shana, and I lived. I squeezed in classes days and nights, weekends and summer for seven years, until I graduated in 1991. I was forty-six.

So many people I have come in contact with over the years—whom the public sees as having it all because they are wealthy, renowned, good-looking, and successful in their careers—are some of the most miserable people you'll ever meet. Their wealth and celebrity haven't helped them create peace and joy. "Restless is the mind. The wind is no wilder," goes the ancient Hindu scripture. I've come to see that success has everything to do with inner peace, which only comes from knowing this truth: No matter what dramas are unfolding in our lives, God's got our back. Stuff happens. In fact, anything we see on the nightly news could have happened to us. But hurtful things, including illnesses, losses, and money and relationship woes, are never for our punishment but for our growth. Life is always slapping us upside our head to awaken us to our calling, so that we will examine our lives, come to know and love ourselves, and grow and change.

Change, change, change. This is the essence of life, and we resist it. Self-reflection—listening to that still, small voice and trusting that what life brings our way is for our healing and betterment—this is the way home to inner peace. It's so simple, but not easy. Like most people, I had to bump my knees, scrape my chin, and get knocked around before realizing the import of paying keen attention to my life. It's still an everyday challenge. My prayer now is that I listen and heed the wisdom of the Spirit before my face hits the floor. I don't want that in my life again. It's not the external that matters—the accessories and accoutrements—it's all about our beliefs and thoughts. It wasn't so easy a road to navigate, learning the importance of taking quiet time each day. I have "monkey mind" when I don't set aside a few minutes each morning for meditation, for sitting still, breathing deeply, and remembering that God's got my back. Without quiet time, I lose my way, my confidence, and my peace. My mind swings to the negative, and I find it jumping from what I should have done to fears about the future. Without meditation and exercise, my life swings off course and I lose my balance and my way. One of my goals is to master my mind and not allow negative things to direct my thoughts, words, or deeds. For me, the commitment to daily communion with God is the key.

When I look back on some of the most painful moments of my life, like the loneliness I felt after the breakup of my first marriage, I realize that it was that very loneliness that led me to books about spirituality, and solitude that allowed me to pursue them in depth. With the inspiration and guidance I gleaned from those books and in Sunday services at Unity—where my decades-long guide, Eric Butterworth, and his wife, Olga, brought wisdom and healing to so many lives—I was able to create more happiness than I had known in the best days of my marriage. So much of who I am today is a result of those experiences.

If our lives were everything we want them to be, everything we dream they should be, what then? Where would our motivation come from without the necessities and challenges that give birth to our inventiveness? The challenges are as fundamental to our existence as gravity, without which our legs would wither away to nothing, leaving us too weak to stand on our own two feet. Struggle strengthens. Strength is a sign of health, and health is the essential physical condition underlying the aesthetics of beauty in all cultures.

I was in my midtwenties, working as the beauty and fashion editor at *Essence*, when I realized how our looks hold us hostage. I had been looking for another way to speak to sisters about our beauty and our bodies. It was the early seventies, and each year the fashion and beauty team would travel to the campus of a historically black college or university to photograph our back-to-school issue. We went to places like Howard University, Dillard, Morgan, and Spelman. I was always seeking gorgeous chocolate women for our pages, to add to the breadth of black beauty I was determined to present in *Essence*. Few black-skinned girls were represented by modeling

agencies, and today some of the beauties who made it into the pages of *Essence* will tell you that I found them on buses, on trains, in restaurants, and walking down New York City streets. It was my goal to celebrate every size, shape, and shade of our women's beauty so we would learn to love what God made, which had been so dishonored and defiled in this Eurocentric culture over the centuries. During those college shoots, I can remember saying to some of the most exquisite-looking sisters walking the campus, or others who'd line up for model go-sees for our photo sessions, "You are so fine, so gorgeous." Inevitably, they would look behind them to see who I was talking to. "You!" I'd insist. And too often they seemed stunned and would say that no one had ever told them they were pretty. Members of their own family—in some cases their own mother—had told them they were too dark, their hair was too short and too kinky, or their nose was too broad and their lips too big.

Though full lips are prized and paid for today, dark skin is still abhorred by many black people—here throughout the Diaspora, and even in our motherland. And each generation passes down the internalized lies, self-loathing, and pain to the next. To not see the beauty in the blackest among us is to slap our ancestral mother in the face, to deny the essence of who we are. It's a shining example of the damage that enslavement, imperialism, and racism have done to our psyches and souls. Healing what's hurting black America—this is what my National CARES Mentoring Movement is dedicated to, and it's specifically what our initiative A New Way Forward is all about. We are taking the healing initiative, created by a brain trust of sixty of the most phenomenal minds, to the people. We are headed for cities throughout the country, or folks can check it out online.

My heart still aches for our young women whose inner beauty is denied and who therefore never have brothers express interest in them for anything other than their bodies. I was raised by my mother, whose values assured I was "Taylor-made" for the beauty and fashion editor position at *Essence*. And there I soon realized that I needed to speak to women about a beauty that was more than just skin deep, that we needed to turn inward. When we do, we tap into the divine source of all that is beautiful, in ourselves and in the world. We radiate it from the inside out, others see it, and we see it in others, whose beauty we had been blinded to. We women, too, are attracted to the superficial—to money, celebrity, and tall, good-looking men. These are all things that are transient, that can be lost in the blink of an eye.

I'm passionate about black people learning to love ourselves, trusting one another, and standing together in unity and strength and about able, stable black people caring for the least able or stable among us—our beleaguered children living in poverty and struggling to survive. Today, 85 percent of black fourth graders are reading below grade level, and 60 percent are functionally illiterate. This is happening on our watch, and we must galvanize our faith institutions, civil rights and sororal and fraternal organizations, block associations, career affinity groups—we need all hands to win the war for the hearts and minds of our young. It's a war between education and catastrophe. Sadly, most of these children will fall into the cycle of generational poverty and be made vulnerable, like the generation before theirs, to the hopelessness, violence, and incarceration that impact the lives of vast numbers of the nation's young people. National CARES is working passionately to help "reculture" our beloved children and gird them against the forces undermining their productivity—including the inability to read well, which dashes academic achievement, and a culture of low expectations and aberrant behaviors, which many youngsters have adopted.

I'm passionate about creating paths to success, literacy, and high achievement so our young won't continue dropping out of schools and filling up prisons. We middle-class and affluent African Americans must reawaken to our power and our moral responsibility. Our love and caring are black children's bridge to a future worth living—and their only hope. We've forgotten who we are and take for granted all that has been made available to us. *This* is not the rough side of the mountain; it was traversed by our ancestors, who pushed ahead, carrying us, their descendants, in their dreams and on their backs, over terrain more treacherous and steep than we will ever know. But I ache for the state of black America today, that we in our turn have let the children, our future, fall by the wayside. And I apologize. To our youngsters who are in peril or otherwise vulnerable, to the many children who we're working for in urban and rural America. My generation has been too quick to criticize and too slow to take responsibility for failing to pass the torch—the knowledge of our glorious history and mighty struggle, the value of education, the power of black love, and the commitment to community and something greater than ourselves. I apologize. For underfunded schools, for allowing war to suck resources from our communities, for providing too few alternatives to war and incarceration, for underpaid teachers in underfunded schools with textbooks that don't inspire and toilets that don' flush. These things are happening on our watch. We who are blessed have abandoned our struggling young, left them to figure things out on their own while we chased the American dream of equal opportunity and conspicuous consumption in the post–civil rights era. In our own self-indulgence, we modeled for them the materialism that shows up today in the ostentatious bling of their artificial diamonds. And few role models have been more ostentatious in this than some of our faith leaders, who are supposed to lead their congregants to secure the young'uns dying outside the sanctuary doors. Chilling numbers of black children are falling through the gaping holes in what should be a safety net that we and our tax dollars provide.

To us able, stable black adults, I say just this: There's no joy and no peace, and there will be none until we learn to serve the least among us. But we have to serve ourselves first. When Gandhi returned to India from South Africa to work with his people to wrest power from the British Empire, he wanted a day off. His people protested: "But, Baba, you can't take a day off, because you're leading this revolution, and we need you here guiding us every day." Gandhi's response lives in my heart: "If I don't take care of me, I won't love you well." And that's where we are. Until we learn to love ourselves, we won't be fully capable of loving and supporting one another—not our mates, our children, or our community.

Learning to love is everyone's calling. National CARES is *heart* work, a work of love and the most important work of my life. I started it as Essence CARES, when I had a lovely paycheck and could afford to buy anything my heart desired. Today I work seven days a week without pay for National CARES, which has devoted leaders recruiting mentors in sixty cities, and I assure you I've never been happier. I'm sixty-five years young and full of joy and energy, and I'm growing new wings. I'm married to the best man I know. I have a loving family. I'm a grandmother. What more could I ask for? I want my people to heal and to take care of the least among us. My unique career path, my history—the painful and shameful parts included—my talents and strengths, these are what allow me to be a bridge between people who have the power to galvanize communities and affect change and those struggling along the margins, whose voices go unheard. I'm not afraid of us. I grew up in the neighborhood, and I'm as comfortable there as I am at the White House. And when I'm at the White House, rest assured I'm there to speak about the needs of our community.

I think my greatest achievement is that I'm awake and present today in ways I wasn't before. I'm not claiming enlightenment just yet, but I see how my life is supposed to be lived. I see what I'm supposed to be giving. I know my calling, my purpose, that it changes over time, and that we always have the capacity to fulfill it. To be able to serve is a blessing. It brings peace. I don't worry like I used to. Worry just makes you sick. And it solves nothing. Every worrisome thing is a call from the Holy Spirit to draw nearer, to look within for peace and solutions. Every problem has a solution. And love is always the answer. More love. More understanding. Getting connected to our deepest self, to the divine that *is* us—all of us. It's the only way home to the happiness and joy we are seeking and deserve. We deserve joy, not pain. We just must learn to put ourselves on our schedule, get still, close out the cacophony in the world—the beeping, buzzing, living online—so we can hear that still, small voice within. Our gifts, our blessings are not just material and physical. The greater ones are on the inside, but society directs us outside ourselves to fill any emptiness we feel within. We are all on the same journey, the journey to our own enchantment—and that door opens inward.

Venus Williams

As the number-twelve all-time top female tennis player, Venus Williams is the winner of three Olympic gold medals and twenty-one Grand Slam titles (seven in singles, twelve in women's doubles, and two in mixed doubles). In 2002, she was the first black female tennis player to be ranked number one in the world.

★

People always ask me when I knew I wanted to be a professional player. As a kid, I didn't think about the future too much, but I always assumed I'd play tennis professionally. My parents told both Serena and me that we'd be number one. They'd say to each of us, "You'll be the best!" They told each of us to pick one tournament and to make it a goal to win it. I picked Wimbledon because historically it's the most prestigious. I didn't miss one tournament—I watched every one. For me, it's always been Wimbledon. I've always wanted to be the best player to play at Wimbledon.

Growing up, we had to work very hard. My dad saw my hometown of Compton, California, as a place where you could see both sides of life and as a place of opportunity because, once you were there, there's only one place you could go, and that was up. We had to bring the best results, meaning that we had to try our hardest every time we stepped foot on the court. We had to be polite. We were told we were the best, and we had to live up to that. Because of that constant reminder, I always believed I *was* the best. On the court, we had to have a positive attitude. My dad would say, "Run for every ball. Even if it's out, run for it!" Every time I went out on the court, I had to believe I was going to win. No matter what. Even if there was someone better across the net, I had to go out there and figure out a way to be better than that person. That was a key part of my strategy in approaching an opponent. If I didn't believe I could beat the opposition, be better than them, then I had lost before I even began.

My family talks all the time about what we learned growing up. I have many great memories. I have four sisters, and we were very close as kids. My dad would sit all five of us down and make us think about life. It's funny to me now because he would ask us pretty tough questions, like "Why does a rich man get richer and a poor man get poorer?" Even though I was only eight years old, his questions helped me to focus. They also taught me to think critically and for myself. My dad taught us not to be afraid of hard work and to relish challenges. My parents encouraged us not to make the same mistakes they'd made. On and off the court, I still call upon those lessons, and they have made all the difference.

I attribute a great deal of my success to having a really supportive family. My family members are my biggest fans, but my sister and I were never judged on how many matches we won or lost. I just had to try my hardest. I had the support of my family either way. I could quit, and they would still love me. I needed that kind of support for the many hurdles and obstacles that came up because I was from such a different background from the other tennis players on the circuit. From the start, coming from Compton, I wasn't supposed to be good at the traditionally elite game of tennis. I had to get past what people said about me, my game, and the untraditional path I had taken. It was especially hard at fourteen or fifteen, when I had to learn to roll with it, somehow not care, and believe in myself.

When I first started playing professionally, I had to put my dad's life lessons into action quickly. I had to develop the ability to get past my mistakes. I had to learn to be responsible for my decisions, especially on the court. If I a lost a match, a huge match, it was no one's fault but my own. I had to figure out what went wrong and then, the next time, pull out something extra from inside myself. I'd tell myself, "You have to play these big matches better." I learned that lesson quickly. And my dad came up with these unbelievable ideas to change the game. He taught us how to think differently, how to be creative on the court, and how to prepare. We spent countless hours playing tennis, but Dad would have us mentally prepare off the court as well. He would have

us visualize what we were going to do and how we were going to win a point. I remember the first time I played at Wimbledon, he told me to go to the stadium court when no one was out there, sit down, and just visualize what it would take for me to win the tournament. He wanted me to visualize match point and how I would handle that pressure and also how I would come back if I was down a break point.

Serena and I were criticized a lot in the beginning because we didn't come up in the country-club circuit and people didn't think my father was doing things the right way, but it didn't bother me. Frankly, I focused on myself and my game. When anyone is critical of what I do, I'm just motivated by it. If someone says I'm not good enough, then I just do better. The criticism has only brought my family together. I believed I could win and that I could play at a championship level. Confidence helped me overcome a lot of criticism and, when I failed, to go back out there and try again. But that confidence was the result of a lot of hard work and focus. I stayed true to my dream, and I avoided the press. I made sure I wasn't around anyone who wasn't positive.

My love of tennis, my desire to be the best at what I do, is what drives me to keep going. I have so much left inside of me and so much more to give. When I came into the game, I was playing it differently from everyone else. I really listened to my dad because he had awesome new ideas about how to play. People say Serena and I changed the game, but actually it was our dad who changed the game behind the scenes. I credit him with helping my sister and me develop a game that was innovative and fresh. He taught us different footwork techniques, how to hit the open-stance two-handed backhand that was pretty much unheard of then, the swinging volleys, and the unbelievable attacking in-your-face game combined with solid defense. It's what has kept us so competitive. And now the game has changed a lot from when I first started playing.

Off the court, I'm interested in fashion. I have my own clothing line, called EleVen, and I love designing. Fashion inspires me to try something different. I like to experiment with fabrics and adornments. I like to see if they'll work on the court, when I'm sweating and diving for balls. You can't be worried about what you're wearing when you're trying to win a big match. It's all about exploring who I am on the inside—from my game to the clothes that I wear when I'm playing it. In fashion, I march to the beat of my own drum, just like I do in my game—but I want to design clothes that other people can wear and relate to.

My greatest achievement is that I lead a positive life. A lot of people can't say that. To be able to live a positive life and to be spiritually balanced are the most important things to me. No matter what you achieve, if you're negative or unhappy, what's the point? When people say, "You inspire me," it makes me happy and it keeps me motivated. For that reason, I hope to be a role model for other people.

My advice to girls who want to be like me is to work hard and believe in yourself—no matter what the next person says. Don't judge yourself by other people's standards, by what color you are, by how much you weigh, or by what you wear. Judge yourself by your own standards. Build a good team around you. If you don't have that in your family, then surround yourself with other people, people who will help you reach your goals, people who are doing positive things in their lives and who want to see you get ahead and succeed. Have fun, and finally, don't stress yourself out. Trust that things will work out.

I can't say whether or not Serena and I have changed the game. I can't gauge the impact we've had. But I do know the number of people watching tennis and the type of people who watch tennis have changed because of us. There still aren't a lot of women of color in professional tennis, which is something I hope changes. I've been fighting for women's rights in tennis, for equal prize money and equal treatment. I'm glad things have begun to progress on those fronts.

I attribute my professional longevity to my spiritual balance and self-discipline. As a young person, you're out there on top of the world. God forbid you lose one match and have everyone on top of you. It's easy to lose perspective. It's hard to be out there in this fast-paced world of celebrity and temptations and not get caught up in drugs or boys or other things that could distract you from your goal. It's hard to be young and under so much pressure. But from the very beginning, when my father first took me out on a tennis court, I was disciplined day in and day out. I was driven from the start, and my father drilled the importance of discipline into me and my sister. It saved me from a lot of the pitfalls that other people experience.

The thing I want people to remember about me is that I was a good person and a great competitor, that I made a difference in my sport. More than the number of tournaments I've won, I hope people see me as a role model. I can't explain how I felt when I won my first Wimbledon. I remember riding back to the hotel in the courtesy car and thinking, "Wow! I just won Wimbledon." Since then, I've won four more times. But winning five times at Wimbledon is not nearly enough for me. I want to win five times, times five. I'm so honored and grateful to play a professional sport at such a high level. It's amazing to be able to do this.

Acknowledgments

I'd first like to thank God, without Whom none of this would be possible.

It took a village to make this book happen: people, places, circumstances, serendipity, luck, begging, and timing all perfectly colliding. I would like to give thanks to all the factors in the universe that played a part in *Inspiration*.

I'd like to thank the women who generously agreed to be a part of *Inspiration*. I'd like to express my gratitude to them for so graciously and honestly sharing their lives, stories, time, loves, losses, and inspirations. I am forever changed by their revelations and the time I shared with them. Not a day passes without me thinking about one of their precious stories. They are all extraordinary human beings.

I'd like to thank my entire family for their love and support throughout my journey: Raymond, for standing beside me with unconditional love. My confidante and sister, Dr. Ruthie McCrary—your energy keeps us all going strong! The Butcher family: David, Alexis, and William. The entire McCrary family. Wiletha McGuire, one of the strongest and most glorious women I have been blessed to know. The Whittakers, the Lewises, the McCrees, the Barringtons, and Deborah Ortiz. To the memory of Monga and Kid, Bernice and Hugh, Kathleen Lewis, Aunt Dores, Aunt Momo, and Aunt Ruth.

Thank you to the many people who helped make this book a reality: Tricia Kallett, thank you so much for introducing and bringing me to Abrams. Your belief and enthusiasm for this book from the very beginning helped bring the project to life. Thank you also to the Klosk family—Craig, Daniel, and especially Molly—for their brilliant assistance. You have a bright future in whatever you choose to do! Thank you to the entire Abrams and Stewart, Tabori & Chang family: Leslie Stoker, thank you for the opportunity and for believing in this book's potential, as well as for understanding the importance of paying tribute to these extraordinary women. Wesley

Royce, you are a talented editor; thank you for your guidance, unwavering support, and patience. Scott Auerbach, thank you so much for helping to keep the project on track. Michael Jacobs, thank you so much for giving *Inspiration* a chance to live.

Crystal Garland, thank you so much for your constant assistance throughout this entire process. You are a true professional and a joy to work with, and you made the creation of this book run infinitely more smoothly from beginning to end. Thank you also to Katie Kennedy for her gracious help. Saleda Bryant, thank you for being there whenever I needed assistance.

Thank you to all my friends, who are daily inspirations, from my lifelong sisters to my new friends: Leslie Danley, Nicole Doss, Nicole Skalski, Carla Diggs Smith, Dena Dodd Perry, Marcia Mackey. Rita Ewing, my first coauthor, and Tonya Lewis Lee, my second coauthor: It was so much fun to create with you both! Lisa Bonner, thank you so much for your support throughout this project. Fran Rauch, thank you for being a friend and a voice of reason. Thank you, Adriene Lopez, for being a friend and supporter for so many years. Thank you, Erica Reid and the entire Reid family—Antonio, Arianna, and Addison—for always opening the peaceful retreat of your home and hearts to me and my family. Thank you to my dear friend Shaun Robinson for always having such a generous heart. Shauna Neely, thank you for your friendship and exquisite jewelry. Thank you to Veronica Webb for being a lifelong friend and a true inspiration. I'd also like to thank Kimberley Hatchett, Cybelle Brown, Jeanine Liburd, and Madeline Nelson for each pushing this book forward in her own special way—your belief in this project has proved invaluable. Thank you to the McIntyres—Everton, Lisa, Taylor, Judah, Madisen, and Megan—for being our family away from home. Thank you, Billy Council, for being a great coach and uncle to Cole, and thank you, Anita Moran, for always being there when Cole, Ella, and I needed you.

Thank you to all the women I admire for their grace, strength, knowledge, fortitude, and friendship: Daryl Roth, Barbara Walters, Marva Smalls, Nancy Lane, Rose Swanson, Susan Taylor, Thelma Golden, Bethann Hardison, Tracy Reese, Iman, Gayle King, Carol Sutton Lewis, Debra Martin Chase, Debra Lee, Terry McMillan, Susan Fales-Hill, and Judy Byrd.

Nathan Hale Williams, thank you so much for the opportunities you created for me, and thank you so much for being a part of *Inspiration*. We have produced some amazing projects together, for which I am deeply grateful.

Lacy Austin, in my feverish search for a photographer, thank you for connecting me with Lauri Lyons. And Lauri, thank you for taking beautiful photographs.

Huge thanks to Sandra Richards and Morgan Stanley Smith Barney for their unwavering support in making this book happen, and to the Studio Museum in Harlem and Mark Bradford, Lunette Iiadom-Boakye, Noel Kirnon, and Elliot Perry, the International Center of Photography, Alvin Ailey American Dance Theater, the Joan Weil Center for Dance, Harlem Children's Zone and Geoffrey Canada, the Children's Defense Fund, the Tracy Reese Flagship Store, American Ballet Theatre, Jana Edelbaum, Soho House New York, Christopher Zunner, Ariel Investments, Act-One, Kevin Dyson and Barney's for great friendship and exquisite clothing, Henry Louis Gates, Kwaku Alston, Sean Joel Johnson, the Four Seasons Hotel Palm Beach, the Beverly Hills Hotel, and the Regent Beverly Wilshire.

Thank you to everyone who helped bring this book to life: Sam Fine; Lloyd Boston; Lisa Sorenson; Terrell Mullin (makeup for Venus Williams); E. J. Johnson; Derrick Thompson; Marcia J. Williams (an incredibly inspiring woman in her own right); Betty Taylor; D'Angelo Thompson (makeup for Soledad O'Brien); Andrea Fairweather Bailey for Fairweather Faces (makeup for Thelma Golden and Judith Jamison); Jackie Sanchez (makeup for Bethann Hardison and Ruby Dee); Dan Bonini for PMK and Iman Home; Larry Sims (hair styling for Laila Ali); Autumn Moultrie (makeup for Keke Palmer and Laila Ali); Jamika Wilson (hair styling for Keke Palmer); Krystal Thorpe for Epiphany Agency; Angie Alvarado for Artists for Higher, Inc. (hair styling and makeup for Raven-Symoné); Kimberly Kimble and D'Andre Michael for the Margaret Maldonado Agency (Mary J. Blige); Valerie Hunt (makeup for Shaun Robinson); Dontay Savoy (hair styling for Shaun Robinson); Nicole Allowitz (styling for Shaun Robinson); Verlyn Antoine (hair styling for Shonda Rhines); Cinzia Zanetti (makeup for Shonda Rhimes); Jaha Johnson; Eric Kaufman; Zuri Edwards; Nora Day; *The Gayle King Show*; *O* magazine; OWN; BET Networks; and Viacom.

To all my teachers and professors from Chrysler Elementary School, Grosse Pointe Academy, Mercy High School, the University of Michigan, and New York University, who taught me the joy of writing. To Vikki, for life and love.

*   *   *

Lauri Lyons would like to acknowledge the special contributions made by the following people toward the completion of this book: Jean and Laurence Lyons, the Black family, and Lacy Austin. Thank you to all the women who graciously contributed their time and support for this project. Thanks to photo assistants Richard Rose, Damian Castro, Erick Bech, Esteban Aladro, and Sam Ortiz; equipment sponsor the International Center of Photography; photography lab sponsor Duggal Visual Solutions, Dave Schroeder, and Heather Gorman; retouching and color correction sponsor: The Beth Schiffer Pro Photo Lab, Helene DeLillo, Shane Connors, and Beth Schiffer; and videographer: Philippe Roc.

Published in 2012 by Stewart, Tabori & Chang
An imprint of ABRAMS

Library of Congress Cataloging-in-Publication Data:
Inspiration : profiles of Black women changing our world / edited by Crystal McCrary and Nathan
Hale Williams ; photographs by Lauri Lyons.
     p. cm.
  ISBN 978-1-58479-959-7
1. African American women—Biography. 2. African American women social reformers—Biography.
3. African American women political activists—Biography. 4. African American women artists—
Pictorial works. 5. African American women—Pictorial works. 6. African American women social
reformers—Pictorial works. 7. African American women political activists—Pictorial works.
8. African American women artists—Pictorial works. 9. Inspiration—Case studies. 10. Social
change—Case studies. I. McCrary, Crystal. II. Williams, Nathan Hale. III. Lyons, Lauri.
  E185.96.I565 2012
  920.72'08996073—dc23   2011031848

Editor: Wesley Royce
Designer: Laura Lindgren
Production Manager: Anet Sirna-Bruder

The text of this book was composed in Simoncini Garamond, Helvetica Neue, and Didot.

Printed and bound in the U.S.A.
10   9   8   7   6   5   4   3   2   1

ABRAMS
THE ART OF BOOKS SINCE 1949
115 West 18th Street
New York, NY 10011
www.abramsbooks.com